***The Uttara Tantra:
A Treatise on
Buddha Nature***

Bibliotheca Indo-Buddhica Series No. 131

# *The Uttara Tantra: A Treatise on Buddha Nature*

A Commentary on
*The Uttara Tantra Ṣāstra*
of Asaṅga

by

**The Venerable**
**Khenchen Thrangu, Rinpoche**
***Abbot of Rumtek Monastery***

**Translated by**
**Ken and Katia Holmes**

Sri Satguru Publications
*A Division of*
**Indian Books Centre**
Shakti Nagar, Delhi
INDIA

*Published by :*
**SRI SATGURU PUBLICATIONS**
Indological & Oriental Publishers
*A Division of*
**Indian Books Centre**
40/5, Shakti Nagar,
Delhi-110007
India



**First Edition : Delhi, 1994**
**ISBN 81-7030-401-6**



## *Acknowledgements*

We would like to thank the many persons who helped make this book possible. First of all we would like to thank Ken and Katia Holmes for translating this book from Tibetan into English. We would also like to thank Jean Johnson, Clarke Fountain, David Reed, and Daniel Pirofsky for help in producing this book. A special thanks to Debra Ann Robinson, Mary McCarry, Tess Evans, Phyllis Ohm, Margot Newman, Katie Haggerty, and Susan Roe who patiently transcribed the tapes of Thrangu Rinpoche's talks.

# Contents

## *Foreword*

India has been the ground for some of the most profound philosophical schools in the world. There is, of course, the Vedic tradition based largely on the Hindu tradition which is one of the world's oldest systems of philosophy. Then there is a more recent philosophical school which began in India around the first century A. D. and ended around the tenth century. This was the time of the flourishing of a school of Buddhism which centered in a dozen monastic universities in Northern India. This school was founded by realized individuals, rather than just scholars, and devoted itself to the examination of reality. These Buddhist practitioners and scholars illuminated the notion that what we conventionally take for real and solid, is not. They developed many logical arguments and demonstrations with the tools they had available to them at the time to show that everything as we perceive it is not as it is but rather an empty of inherent existence (Skt. śūnyatā). What we take for "reality" is, for the most part, a projection of our mind.

This philosophical tradition which became known as mahāyāna Buddhism spread throughout the Far East but has been largely ignored in our modern, scientific age. This, however, is ironic because now physicist working on the frontiers of subatomic theory have basically come up with the notion that nothing is solid, but rather is almost completely empty space with certain energy relations between them. Furthermore, if we even try to apply simple logic to these "building blocks" of matter such as electrons, we have to conclude that these elementary particles do not exist in any single place and can only be described in terms of probability of where they might be and in their relationship to the rest of the material of the universe. Even in our more down-to-earth sciences we are discovering that objects which we thought of as distinct objects such as a single tree in a forest must be thought of as a complex organic combination with highly complicated interactions with the surrounding environment and not as a single unit.

What does this mean to the ordinary individual? It means that for us to gain any understanding of why we were placed on this earth and how we should live our life now we are here, we have to examine this world to see what is lasting and enduring, and what is just a transitory display of phenomena. The Madhyamaka school with great masters such as Nāgārjuna, Asaṅga, Vasubandhu, Chandrakīrti, Dignāga, Nāropa, Śhāntarakṣhita, Śhāntideva did just this. They demonstrated that our suffering and problems and confusion in this world is due to our almost innate belief that we are a self as a solid enduring object.

Unfortunately, with the confusion after the Moslem invasion of India a vast amount of this literature was lost in India and only fragments of it remain in Sanskrit. However, a large portion of this literature was translated into Tibetan and written down and studied and practiced in Tibet. Because of this one of the greatest works of this tradition, The *Uttara Tantra* by the great scholar Asaṅga was preserved. This book consists of 404 verses devoted almost exclusively to enduring and permanent in this world, namely, tathāgatagarba or buddha nature. Buddha nature is that primary essence that all beings possess and which is the essence that makes it possible for all beings to achieve enlightenment. The *Uttara Tantra* is considered so important in the Tibetan tradition that these root verses are often memorized. In addition this text is also extremely relevant for all Buddhist practitioners because it answers many questions such as how can one tell if someone is enlightened and what are the necessary qualities to achieve enlightenment.

In the late 1970s Kagyu Samye Ling in Scotland invited the Venerable Thrangu Rinpoche to come to Europe and teach. Thrangu Rinpoche was eminently qualified because he had just finished establishing the curriculum for the Kagyu lineage of Tibetan Buddhism for its head, the sixteenth Gyalwa Karmapa. He chose one of the most important texts of Tibetan Buddhism to begin with and spent several months giving a line by line commentary on this *Uttara Tantra*.

The *Uttara Tantra* like many texts of the time was written in very terse, compact language with extremely deep and subtle references which makes the text accessible to only an extremely erudite scholar. This book follows an oral tradition used by lamas for the last ten centuries which meant that every point was numbered, placed in a category, stated, restated, emphasized, and then summarized. Had the transcripts simply been typeset, the commentary would have been about 700 pages long and would have been very difficult to follow. So with the help of chapters, headings, and extensive elimination of repetition and categorization, the *Uttara Tantra* was brought down to a manageable size which could be easily read by Westerners. At the suggestion of Ken Holmes the numbers of the verses in the *Changeless Nature* were added in brackets before the corresponding paragraphs of the commentary so one can read the verses of the *Changeless Nature* and then read the corresponding commentary. A glossary and appendix of Tibetan terms were also added for the reader not familiar with Buddhist terms. An attempt was also made to make the commentary so that the reader could read it without having to refer to the root text.

The result is quite extraordinary. We have a complete rendering of an intact text of the period by someone who not only has studied it for a lifetime, but who has done the same meditative practices that Asaṅga did to reach the realization described in the text. In addition to this we have Thrangu Rinpoche's line by line exposition explaining every word of the text. The covering of a text with this precision with the guide of Jamgon Kongtrul's śhāstra which has to be one of the greatest commentaries on any religious text of this period is something which has been available to only a few rare individuals living over the past centuries in monasteries in Tibet.

Clark Johnson,Ph. D.
December 21, 1993

# Chapter 1

## *An Introduction to the Uttara Tantra*

The Buddha gave many teachings and these teachings are classified into three turnings of the wheel of dharma. The subject matter of the first turning of the wheel of dharma are the four noble truths. These truths are the truth of suffering, the truth of the origin of suffering, the truth of the cessation of suffering, and the truth of the path. The teachings of this first turning were aimed at individuals who did not have the sharpest intelligence and needed teachings that were easier to comprehend. In this turning the Buddha stated there was suffering, that the defilements were the cause of suffering, and there was a possibility for the liberation from all of this. Everything in this turning was phrased in terms of something tangible and in terms of conventional reality or relative truth. In the second turning the Buddha took a different position by explaining that everything that appears to exist actually does not have this reality. In this turning the Buddha said, "There is no form, no sound, no smell, no taste" etc. (as in the *Prajñā-pāramitā* or the *Heart* sūtra) showing that all the objects of the senses and all the forms of appearance are simply illusory and have no ultimate reality. So, the actual nature of all phenomena is voidness.

In the second turning the Buddha established that all phenomena are void but this point was not elucidated.

However, in the third turning, the Buddha revealed the ultimate nature of phenomena by showing that this voidness was not a total absence, a total emptiness of everything, but has qualities of the ultimate nature of phenomena. These teachings also show that all beings possess the essence of the Buddha. If they work on the path, they will be able to develop the perfect knowledge of the Buddha. The *Uttara Tantra* explains that this essence of Buddhahood is present in the mind of all beings. After the teachings of the third turning, many works were composed by learned teachers which pertained to this same subject matter. For example, the *bodhisattva* Maitreya composed five teachings on this topic.

### *This Commentary*

The *Uttara Tantra* is one of the five teachings of Maitreya and is related to the third turning. This text on the *Uttara Tantra* is based on the commentary by Jamgon Kongtrul Rinpoche and has two main parts. The first part is a general introduction which covers the nature of the text, the author, how it was composed, and so forth which is reviewed in this chapter.[1] The second part of the commentary is on the actual text itself and is divided into eight points.

The first point is that there are two kinds of Buddhist teachings—the words of the Buddha (*sūtras*) and the commentaries composed by others on the Buddha's works

[1]The *Uttara Tantra* is śāstra by Maitreya on the dharanisvaranraja *sūtra* of the Buddha. Thrangu Rinpoche used the commentary by Jamgon Kongtrul (1813-1899) which has not been translated into English for the basis of this exposition. The root text has been translated by Kèn and Katia Holmes as *The Changeless Nature*.

(*śāstras*). One might think the *Uttara Tantra* is composed of the words of the Buddha because Maitreya is a representative of the Buddha. However, this work is related to the subject matter taught in the third turning and therefore it is classified as an explanatory text composed by someone other than the Buddha.

Secondly, what source did the *Uttara Tantra* rely on? Some claim this teaching is related to the Mind Only (Skt. Cittamātra) school, but this is not so because this teaching relates directly to the teachings on absolute truth. The *Uttara Tantra* derives its subject matter from all the sūtras of the three turnings---it is like the quintessence of all these sūtras and particularly it has a close connection to one sūtra taught at the request of King Iśvara.

The third point examines the authorship of this work. In general, the śāstras are produced by authors who have one of three qualifications. The best is one who has a direct understanding of the absolute truth of phenomena. If someone does not have this understanding, then second best is someone who has met face-to-face with a deity such as Mañjuśri. The poorest are those authors who are well educated and only have a thorough knowledge of the five branches of the sciences (grammar, logic, craftsmanship, healing, and spirituality). Texts written by someone who doesn't have one of the above three qualifications aren't worthy of a Buddhist commentary. Maitreya, the author of the *Uttara Tantra,* is even better than the best category because not only did he possess realization of absolute truth, but he was a *bodhisattva* of the highest level.

The fourth point discusses how this work spread after Maitreya had given the teachings of the *Uttara Tantra*. Buddha Śākyamuni had actually made a prediction that there would be a teaching given by one of the highest bodhisattvas and it would relate to the highest possible meaning and these teachings would be given to men and propagated among them.

### *The Story of Asaṅga*

The story of the spread of the *Uttara Tantra* begins at the famous Buddhist University of Nālandā in India. The university was set on fire by heretics and many precious teachings were destroyed including most of the Abhidharma teachings. At that time a nun called Salwai Tsultim became very worried that the teachings would be lost. So she decided to have sons to allow the teachings to grow and spread again. She had two sons: Asaṅga who became a proponent of the *mahāyāna* teachings and Vasubandhu who became an outstanding proponent of the *hīnayāna* teachings.

Asaṅga began by meditating very diligently on Maitreya. He practiced for three years and didn't seem to be getting any results. He became very depressed at not having accomplished anything in his meditation. So he left his retreat and on the way met a man who was rubbing a rock. He inquired and found that the man was rubbing the rock to get rid of it because the rock was blocking the sun from shining on his house. Asaṅga was so impressed by his perseverance that he decided to try again. He returned and meditated for 12 years and still did not feel he was getting anywhere with his meditation and became depressed again. He left his retreat and on the way he saw a dog which was very sick and thin. The dog was very angry and ready to bite him. Suddenly, Asaṅga felt strong compassion for the dog because he noticed that the dog had worms in his wounds. He wanted to remove the worms to help the dog, but realized that if he pulled the worms off, he would kill them. It was a choice between killing the worms or leaving the worms on the dog which would cause the dog to die. But Asaṅga felt such strong compassion and felt that he must find a way to get the worms out. He thought, "If I take the worms off with my tongue, then the worms won't be hurt and the dog will get better." So he leaned down and stuck out his tongue; and as he touched the ground, Maitreya appeared before him. He saw Maitreya and exclaimed, "How is it possible! I have been practicing this meditation for 12 years and haven't been able to meet you. You really don't have much compassion for me." Maitreya said, "It wasn't my lack of compassion. I was there the whole time but you couldn't see me because you had too many obscurations. After 12 years of practice, your obscurations had become so slight that when you saw the dog, you were able to have compassion and to see me." After their meeting, Maitreya and Asaṅga went to the Tuṣita buddha-field and there Maitreya gave teachings on the second turning to Asaṅga. From these teachings and especially the teachings of the *Prajñāpāramitā* Asaṅga composed the *Abhisamayālaṅkāra*. Maitreya also gave teachings on the third turning with some related to the relative meaning and some related to the absolute meaning of the *dharma*. Three teachings pertained to the relative meaning: the *Mahāyānasūtrālaṅkāra*, the *Dharmatāvibhaṅga*, and the *Madhyāntavibhaṅga*. The teachings related to the absolute meaning of reality were the *Abhisamayālaṅkāra* and the *Uttara Tantra* śāstra. So Maitreya gave Asaṅga these five teachings and they were transmitted to human beings of our world.

The fifth point discusses the line of transmission of the *Uttara Tantra*. The teachings of Maitreya were transmitted in two lines—the words and the meaning. The *Uttara Tantra* was given to Asaṅga and he transmitted it to his brother Vasubandhu. Later Asaṅga wrote five works on the five transmissions from Maitreya to make Maitreya's teachings more accessible to everyone. His brother Vasubandhu also wrote commentaries on two of these five works of Maitreya. He wrote a commentary on the *Dharmatāvibhaṅga* and the *Madhyāntavibhaṅga.*

Among these five teachings, three were disseminated quite widely. These were the *Abhisamayālaṅkāra*, the *Madhyāntavibhaṅga*, and the *Mahāyānasūtrālaṅkāra* and were transmitted by Vasubandhu to his disciple Diṅnāga. Diṅnāga passed them to his disciple Lodro Tenpa who disseminated these teachings quite widely. The other two teachings, the *Uttara Tantra* and the *Dharmatāvibhaṅga*, were more profound and were given to only a few pupils.

In Tibet there were two periods of history in which the Buddhist teachings were widely spread. The earlier period during the eighth century at the time of King Thrisong Deutsen or the "time of the three," with the "three" being *mahāpaṇḍita* Śāntarakśita, King Thrisong Deutsen, and Guru Padmasambhava. During this time these first three teachings of Maitreya were translated into Tibetan and disseminated widely. The two profound works were hidden treasures (Tib. *terma*[2]) and were hidden so that they were not known during this first period. Much later Maitripa, one of Marpa's gurus, saw a *stūpa* that was cracked and

[2] Tibetan words in this text are spelled as they are pronounced, not as they are spelled in Tibetan. Their Tibetan spelling can be found in Appendix A.

from the stūpa came a brilliant light. Maitripa became curious and found these two texts inside the crack. He found their meaning was so deep that he wasn't sure he understood them. So he prayed to Maitreya for blessings to understand these texts and Maitreya appeared to him and gave him the ritual reading (Tib. *lung*). After that reading Maitripa could understand the text clearly. These teachings were then passed on to many *paṇḍitas* or the great scholars in India.

Later these deeper teachings spread in Tibet. There were two main lines of transmission—the transmission of the words and the transmission of the meaning of the text. The words were transmitted mainly by Loden Sherab. He was a translator who went to a preeminently Muslim part of India where he received the teachings of the *Uttara Tantra* and the *Dharamatāvibhāga* and translated them into Tibetan. His approach followed that of the Madhyamaka school. At the same time there was another lama named Senka Uche who received the teachings of the *Uttara Tantra* from the Indian teacher, Guru Tsatsana. He meditated on it to understand its deep meaning and started the meditation transmission.

The main difference between the scholarly and the meditative approach is that in the meditative approach "voidness" is not understood as the absence of everything, but as containing the essence of Buddhahood. In the meditative approach, however, one meditates on the voidness as containing the essence of Buddha to understand this concept. This tradition combined the theoretical material of the *Uttara Tantra* with meditation of *mahāmudrā*. This tradition based on the five teachings of Maitreya was passed on to the third Karmapa, Rangjung

Dorje. He wrote a short summary of the *Uttara Tantra* and through him the *Uttara Tantra* was transmitted to all the main lamas of the Kagyu lineage. For example, this teaching was transmitted to the eighth Shamarpa Rinpoche, Chuji Dondrup, and to the eighth Tai Situpa Rinpoche, Chuji Jungne, and to Jamgon Kongtrul.

The sixth point concerns the subject matter of the *Uttara Tantra*. As mentioned before, the Buddha gave his teachings in three turnings of the wheel of dharma. All his teachings, however, have a similar root with the essential point being the absence of a "self." Some religions believe that if one does what pleases God or the gods, then they will be rewarded one and one will obtain greater happiness. They also believe that if one does something that goes against God or the gods, one will encounter misfortunes and fall into a lower realm. There is no such belief in the Buddhist teachings. What happens to one is not the result of pleasing or displeasing a god. The Buddha's teachings are based on the study of the nature of things, so when the nature of phenomena is completely understood, one has attained Buddhahood. If one does not understand the nature of things, one continues to live in conditioned existence (Skt. *saṃsāra*).

The key to all Buddhist teachings is the twofold absence of self and of phenomena. Normally, we believe that we are a separate "self" and this belief in a "self" arises from the idea of "I." As soon as we think "I" or "myself," there develops the wish to keep this "I" happy and comfortable which gives rise to desire. We want to provide that "I" with all the happiness we can find. Then when this "I" feels threatened, the threat generates anger. This "I" will also feel it is better and has better qualities than others and this will generate pride. If this "I" fears there are others who are as good or better, then jealousy will be generated. To summarize, as soon as there is this belief that the individual self has a reality, then all the five negative afflictions (Skt. *kleśas*) of desire, anger, aversion, pride, and jealousy are generated. The belief in the existence of phenomena is a consequence of the first belief. When we believe we exist, then we also believe that all phenomena one experiences also exists.

The main point of Buddhist practice is to eliminate the belief of self and phenomena. The way to eliminate the belief in self is to investigate the location of the one who thinks "I am." If one thinks "I," then who is thinking "I"? Then try to find this "I" somewhere. If one meditates on this and investigates it closely, one will not find anything that is called the "I." Through this process one will understand the nonexistence of self. The belief in the existence of phenomena which appears to be real and substantial is more difficult. But when one considers it more closely, one will begin to see that phenomena are very much like a bubble in water or a dream. All these things do not have any solid reality either.

To summarize, the main point of all three turnings of the wheel of dharma is to understand the nonexistence of self and of phenomena. The absence of a "self" is voidness (*śūnyatā*), but this voidness is not to be misunderstood as blankness, a complete emptiness. It is not like empty space because empty space is frozen and no change can manifest from it. Śūnyatā has a different quality. This voidness is by nature clarity (Tib. *salwa*). Having the nature of clarity means that when beings are still impure, all the various appearances of phenomena can manifest within this clarity.

When individuals have eliminated their impurities, Buddhahood is manifested in clarity. Within this clarity the forms (Skt. *kāyas*) of the Buddha and the activity of the Buddha can manifest. So this voidness is full of all these possibilities. For everything to manifest in the impure and the pure phase, this voidness must be indivisible from clarity. The clarity represents the very vivid intelligent aspect. So clarity and emptiness are completely united and the union of these two is the essence of all Buddhas and is present within the mind of all beings. If one can realize the unity of clarity and voidness, one can reach Buddhahood. This essence of Buddhahood is present in all beings without any distinction which means that whoever practices can realize and reach Buddhahood. There is no difference between a man and a woman, or of a race or social class or anything else because everyone has this essence of enlightenment.

The reason one does not realize the essence of enlightenment is that it is obscured by defilements. One can distinguish three stages of defilements. In the impure phase, the stage of ordinary beings, buddha nature is totally obscured by defilements. In the second phase of the bodhisattvas the impurities are slightly purified with the obscurations partly removed. Finally, in the phase of total purity one is a Buddha.

The concept of buddha nature is central to the Buddhist teachings and is sometimes referred to by the Sanskrit word *gharba* which means "the inner core of something." If one has a grain with a husk, the essential part of the grain is called the "gharba." The parallel is that human beings have the essence of Buddha in them, but it is covered by fleeting impurities. This kernel, buddha nature is the main topic of the *Uttara Tantra.*

The seventh point discusses the different ways of presenting the teachings. As we mentioned before, there is the tradition of Loden Sherab based on the more intellectual approach connected with the Madhyamaka tradition. The second approach which came from Śākya Dorje is the tradition of the immediate apprehension of the subject matter through meditation. This latter approach is the more direct approach in which one meditates on the mahāmudrā and the actual meaning of the nature of phenomena.

### *Name of the Text*

Most Tibetan texts translated from Sanskrit give the Sanskrit name and the Tibetan name in the title. They also usually contain a salutation by the translator to an emanation of the Buddha in order to receive the blessing of the Buddha so the translation will go forward without any obstacles. After the title and salutation, the *Uttara Tantra* begins with the actual words of Maitreya.

The *Uttara Tantra* was originally written in Sanskrit which is called "the language of the gods." This work was then translated into Tibetan to make it accessible to Tibetans who could then read, contemplate, and meditate on it. The name of the text is in both Sanskrit and Tibetan to remember the kindness of the translators who made the work available to the Tibetan people and to show that the work was an original Sanskrit source taught directly by the Buddhas or bodhisattvas. The name of the text is first given in Sanskrit and is called the *Mahāyāna Uttara Tantra Śāstra*. Then it is translated into Tibetan as *tegpa chenpo gyu lama tan cho* which in English would literally be "the ultimate mahāyāna treatise on continuity." Taking each word, *tegpa* literally means to "carry" or "lift." This word "carry" has two different aspects: the process aspect of carrying and the result aspect of carrying. The process aspect is represented by the path of the bodhisattva. The result aspect is reaching the state of Buddhahood. The word "*tegpa*" or "*yāna*" in Sanskrit, can be either small or great and here it refers to the great aspect. Mahāyāna in Sanskrit means "great yāna" or "great action of carrying." It is great for seven different reasons, some of which are as follows: the aim of the path is great (or very wide), the diligence used on the path is great, the *jñāna* or knowledge used on the path is very great.

Following "*tegpa chenpo*" is "*gyu lama.*" The Sanskrit word for "*gyu lama*" is "uttara tantra" and this is usually the short name given to this work. *Uttara Tantra* can be explained from the viewpoint of the literal words or from the viewpoint of the terminology of its meaning.

From the terminology viewpoint, the first word *gyu* means "continuity" and means there is a continuity in the words and the continuity of these words creates a clear understandable meaning which makes up the work. To this word "*gyu*" is added the qualifier *lama* which means "ultimate," "superior," "higher" or "excellent." This is added to "continuity" because the continuity of this text contains the deepest meaning.

From the viewpoint of meaning of the work, the word "*gyu*" means "continuity" but in this context it means the continuity of the essence of the Buddhahood which never changes whether it is in terms of the ground when it is present in all beings, or in terms of the path when beings are practicing the attainment of enlightenment, or in terms of fruition when one becomes a Buddha. Throughout all these phases the nature of Buddhahood remains the same so there is an unbroken continuity all along its development. The word "*lama*" here means "ultimate" or "highest" because the type of practice which will come from this text is not ordinary Buddhist practice, but superior to the practice of hīnayāna. It is a very high type of practice because it points to the ultimate nature of all phenomena. It also comes from a very high bodhisattva which is another reason for giving it the qualifier of "ultimate." Finally, the word "ultimate" is in the title because the *Uttara Tantra* involves explaining absolute truth so it is like a bridge between the sūtras and the tantras.

The last word "*tan cho*" or "śāstra" in Sanskrit literally means "a teaching which brings remedy" or a remedial teaching. This is because these teachings which are elucidations of the Buddha's teachings constitute a remedy for all the defilements and help beings abandon the sufferings of the three dimensions of existence.

The names of Buddhist works are generally given because of an analogy or an example. Here the name *gyu* is given in reference to the subject matter of the work which is the essence of Buddhahood. This continuity refers to the subject matter and also the function of the work. The function of this work is to help beings enter the Mahāyāna path.

### *The Salutation*

The salutation of the translators to the Buddhas is "homage to all the Buddhas and bodhisattvas." The Tibetan word for

Buddha is *sang gay* and each syllable illustrates that the Buddha has two qualities: the quality of purity because he has eliminated all negative impurities and the quality of realization because once the impurities are gone, there is the full understanding of everything. The first syllable *sang* means "totally purified" or "awakened." meaning awakened from the sleep of ignorance. A Buddha has completely eliminated all impurities, all the things that had to be removed have been removed. The second part of the word *gay* means "fully blossomed" referring to the fact that once every obscuration has been fully removed, the pure intelligence of a Buddha understanding all phenomena with full clarity. This word *gay* is also used to describe what happens to a lotus flower when it opens up completely. So the word *sang gay* in this context means awakened and fully blossomed.

The next word in the salutation is "bodhisattvas" or *chang chub sem pa*. This word was translated from the Sanskrit into four syllables in Tibetan. Literally, it means "those who have enough courage to strive for enlightenment." So the first word *chang chub* or "enlightenment," can be broken into *chang* which means "completely purified" which has essentially the same meaning as *sang* in Tibetan and means purified of all ignorance. *Chub* means internalized or assimilated. This means that once all the obscurations have been removed, all knowledge has been realized. The Tibetan word *changchub* is the word for "enlightenment" in general, but in this particular context of bodhisattvas it means "almost completely purified" or "has almost completely assimilated the meaning of everything." The second word *sempa* means "those who have the courage to embark on the path of enlightenment." So in the salutation the translators prostrate to the Buddhas and bodhisattvas in order to receive the blessings so their work will be done properly and without difficulties.

### *Divisions of the Commentary*

Following the salutation the text by Maitreya begins. Buddhist commentaries usually follow the style of presenting the work in three main divisions. Usually, each chapter begins with one verse which is a condensed summary of the whole chapter, followed by a set of verses giving detailed explanations of each of the points mentioned in the first part, and a third set recapitulating the meaning of the verses. This first introductory chapter has three parts. Part A of the first division shows the work is composed of seven points called "indestructible" or *vajra* points because they are very profound like a vajra. Part B shows this work is connected with the sūtras and is based on Buddha's teachings. Part C is an explanation of the order of the seven points.

As already mentioned, all beings want to find some kind of happiness and eliminate their difficulties. In this respect everyone is the same. The difference between individuals lies in the way they go about attaining this happiness. Some people seek material happiness and some try to find happiness through the dharma. Those who try to find worldly happiness might believe happiness will come to them by achieving fame or success or wealth. If they try this, they will not reach real happiness. The only way to find true happiness is to achieve Buddhahood. When one is a Buddha, all negative things which could bring unhappiness have been relinquished and everything that is to be realized has been realized. Only then can eternal happiness be achieved. All other attempts will bring temporary happiness. So the first points examined in the *Uttara Tantra* relate to this goal.

### *Outline of the Work*

[1][3] The first three points of the *Uttara Tantra* relate to the Buddha, the dharma, and the *saṅgha* because these lead to the goal of enlightenment. The first vajra point is the Buddha who shows the way to enlightenment. The second vajra point is the dharma which are the teachings given by the Buddha and show us how to attain our goal. The third vajra point is the saṅghạ or our companions on the path who help us from straying from the path. These three vajra points are external causes. Besides this we need something within ourself. If we don't have anything within that makes it possible to reach enlightenment, then we cannot actually reach it. The fourth vajra point is the essence of Buddhahood called buddha nature which is present in all beings. Once we know buddha nature is present in the mind of all beings, we know that whoever strives for enlightenment can attain it. We cannot say this person can reach Buddhahood, but that person can't because all persons have the seed of enlightenment. But it is not enough to have the seed of enlightenment; we must cultivate it so it develops fully into Buddhahood. We must exert ourself to remove all impurities for the goal to be

[3] The numbers in brackets are the verse numbers of the original text. They may be found in The Changeless Nature text.

achieved and this effort is the fifth vajra point. Then the good qualities achieved after obtaining enlightenment make up the sixth vajra point.

Why is it important to reach enlightenment? It is important because it is a state of possessing all the qualities which are the ultimate fulfillment for oneself. All that is left are all perfect qualities wh· ·h are not just of value for oneself, but automatically have great value for all other beings trapped in conditioned existence. The seventh and last vajra point, then, is the activity of a Buddha. This activity flows naturally from Buddhahood to benefit all other beings.

### *The Connection to the Sūtras*

[2] These seven vajra points were not arbitrarily made up by Maitreya, but were taught by the Buddha in the sūtras. The Buddha taught this subject in seven vajra points because there is an inner connection between these points and their intrinsic characteristics. The Buddha taught this relationship at the request of King Iśvara in the *Dhāraniśvarāraja* sūtra. In the introductory chapter of that sūtra there is a teaching on the three jewels (the Buddha, the dharma, and the saṅgha). The Buddha is shown to be the one who has reached full realization of the true nature of all phenomena. From this realization springs the dharma. Once there is this teaching of the Buddha, there are persons who accompany the Buddha and learn his teachings and train their minds and become the saṅgha.

In the *Dhāraniśvarāraja* sūtra the other four vajra points are covered beginning with how bodhisattvas can learn to purify the obstacles blocking the way to realization. They have to purify emotional afflictions and their dualistic thinking which is blocking true wisdom. This sūtra explains the ways one can eliminate these obscurations. If the essence of Buddhahood is purified, then it manifests. This sūtra shows 60 different ways that the essence of Buddhahood can be made pure and manifest. The fifth vajra point, enlightenment, is introduced by explaining the 16 aspects of compassion of a bodhisattva. With enlightenment all the qualities inherent in enlightenment are present (such as the ten powers of the Buddha and the four fearlessnesses.) The sixth vajra point is the qualities of enlightenment. The seventh vajra point describes the activity of the Buddha or the natural outflow of activities of Buddhahood. These points are in this particular order to show the intimate connection between them. The seven vajra points are also taught in several other sūtras, but they are not taught in sequence and the connection between the points is not discussed in the other sūtras.

### *The Order of the Vajra Points*

[3] When the Buddha enters the world, he is the root of all the good qualities, of all the forms of true happiness. Logically, the first vajra point has to be the Buddha from whom all the good qualities and happiness spring. Once a Buddha has entered the world to help other beings, he turns the wheel of dharma. From the Buddha springs the dharma. Once the dharma exists, it spreads. When beings are ready to understand the dharma, they practice the dharma each according to their ability and the aspect of the path that suits them. Through the practice of the path, they develop

signs of realization and become known as "realized saṅgha" which is the third vajra point.

When the Buddha, the dharma, and the saṅgha are present, there is the possibility of realizing the existence of buddha nature. Although persons possess buddha nature from the beginning of time, the presence of the three jewels makes it possible for individuals to learn about Buddhahood so that they can begin making buddha nature manifest. They learn how to purify the obscurations that cover it. Little by little this essence of Buddhahood becomes clearer and clearer until the wisdom (jñāna) manifests completely. But for this to happen there must be the external conditions of the Buddha, the dharma, and the saṅgha and the inner condition of buddha nature within one's mind. With the combination of the external and internal conditions, it is possible to remove all the impurities obscuring the essence of Buddhahood. Once all these impurities have been removed, one achieves Buddhahood which is the connection between the fourth and the fifth vajra point.

Once Buddhahood is achieved, one asks the question of what qualities are connected with this condition and this question is answered in the sixth vajra point. When one achieves Buddhahood, it is not only great fulfillment for oneself, but also of great value to others. The value for oneself means the qualities of enlightenment pertain not only to the body aspect, but to the mind aspect. The qualities of the body will be explained in terms of the two kāyas of the Buddha (*nirmāṇakāya* and *sambhogakāya*). The qualities of the mind are all the qualities of the *dharmakāya.*

Once the qualities of Buddhahood are present, great benefit for all other beings springs from them automatically which brings about the seventh vajra point, the activities of Buddhahood. So from these qualities comes the activities of the Buddha which help all beings. This activity is totally effortless, continuing until saṃsāra has been completely eliminated.

The above three parts were an explanation of the central structure of the text which in Tibetan is referred to as the "body" of the text. What follows are the different parts or what Tibetan scholars call the "limbs" of the text. The detailed explanation of the seven vajra points is actually divided into two sections: the goal one is aiming for which covers the first three vajra points plus a summary, and the tools for reaching enlightenment which comprise the remaining four vajra points.

# CHAPTER 2

## *The Buddha*

The explanation of the Buddha is divided into three sections: a description of what a Buddha is by means of the salutation, a section describing the qualities of the Buddhas, and a section with a more detailed explanation of these qualities.

### *The Salutation*

[4] The Buddha is described in the salutation. A Buddha is someone who has reached total fulfillment. Buddhahood is the ultimate fulfillment for oneself because it is free from all suffering and all possibility of suffering. If one is a Buddha, there is no longer any fear, any worry, or any doubt that suffering will never return. When Buddhahood has been achieved, one does not selfishly enjoy it just for oneself but from this Buddhahood springs activity which spontaneously helps all other beings. In the text the salutation is made in the form, "I bow down..." and lists six qualities of Buddhahood. The first three qualities of the Buddha are connected to the value to oneself and the last three qualities are connected to the value for others.

The first quality of Buddhahood is the quality of being uncreated and not composed of anything. The text says the Buddha is eternal, centerless, and endless. Eternal means there is no birth or starting point of the Buddha. Centerless means there is no place where the Buddha abides. Endless means there is no death, no interruption of the Buddha. A birth, a place of abiding, and an ending, implies a condition of change. If there were change, even with happiness in the beginning, this happiness could change to suffering. Change automatically means impermanence and impermanence implies suffering. Being uncreated, the Buddha doesn't belong to conditioned phenomena which changes.

The second quality of Buddhahood is peace or equanimity which implies the spontaneous presence of everything beneficial. This peace means that all of the conceptual agitation has totally ended. One is constantly agitated by millions of thoughts so the mind is never peaceful. We must exert effort all the time with everything being difficult and a trouble. Whatever one wants is not available because there is always something in the way. This creates mental pain and physical difficulties because one is always struggling to do things not once, but again and again. In contrast, the Buddha with this peace of mind doesn't need to make any effort and everything happens spontaneously and effortlessly.

The third quality of Buddhahood is that it relies on no external conditions. The essence of Buddhahood is inherent, so one cannot give Buddhahood to another. Also one can't look outside oneself to become enlightened. Buddhahood realizes itself and has nothing to do with an external process.

The above three qualities are related to value for oneself. From the presence of these qualities springs the next three qualities of value for others. When Buddhahood is achieved, one has gone beyond suffering and all the causes of suffering. In other words, one is awakened from ignorance and this is the achievement of ultimate happiness. There is this full understanding of the nature of all phenomena which is the full blossoming of jñāna. When this happens, a Buddha has the power to help others and shows other beings the fearless path. To do this he or she has a quality of knowledge which comes from complete realization of the nature of everything and the quality of compassionate love which creates a desire to share this knowledge with others.

Compassion and knowledge are compared to a sword and a vajra. The sword cuts through all suffering. The vajra destroys the wall of doubts which is surrounded by the thicket of wrong views. So the Buddha uses compassion and knowledge to rid beings of their suffering, wrong views, and misunderstandings. The three qualities of a Buddha connected to the value for others are wisdom, compassion, and the power to help others.

The short answer to the qualities of the Buddha is perfect fulfillment for oneself and for others. A longer answer is to list the above six qualities. The most complete answer is to say the Buddha has eight qualities which are the six qualities plus the value for self and value for others. It is beneficial for the Buddhist practitioner to learn these eight qualities and to keep them in mind, not just read them in the text.

### *Qualities of the Buddha*

The first quality of the Buddha is "uncreated" (Tib. *du ma che*) which also means "unconditioned" in Tibetan. One part of the Tibetan word means "gathered" or "gathered together." It is gathered together by many different causal conditions that make up things. For example when growing a flower, we first need the seed which is the basic cause for the existence of the flower. We also need a whole set of secondary conditions such as water, fertilizer, and heat that makes growth of the flower possible. The developed flower therefore is not "unconditioned" because it is a result of the seed and all the factors needed for its growth. We may ask what is wrong with something being created from a composite of many different things. The problem is that if one of the factors is lacking, then the object won't develop or come about. For instance, if water is lacking, the flower will wither and die or if heat is lacking, the flower will not bloom. In contrast, the the essence of Buddhahood is not created by different causes or conditions. The essence of Buddhahood is present in the mind of all beings from the beginning. Because it was not created, the nature of Buddhahood is changeless.

The second quality of the Buddha is the spontaneous presence of all the good qualities of the Buddha. This spontaneity means the absence of effort. All the qualities of the Buddha, the qualities of the purity of the dharmakāya and form kāyas are inherently present and do not have to be modified or developed in any way. They have always been there without any effort.

The third quality is realization without relying on some external condition. If one had to rely on something external, one would be controlled by external circumstances to realize it. The Buddha has no need to rely on an external object or condition. One may ask, "What is doing this realizing to become a Buddha?" It is the jñāna, the aspect of the pure intelligence of the mind. This jñāna recognizes itself without the introduction of any outside factor so enlightenment becomes a process of jñāna seeing its own nature.

The next three qualities are connected with value for others. The fourth quality is perfect knowledge. If one shows the path to others, one needs to know it oneself; otherwise there is nothing to show. This means the understanding of the Buddha cannot be partial and the Buddha must continuously perceive the true nature of all phenomena, not just glimpse it. The perfect knowledge of the Buddha has two aspects: the knowledge of seeing phenomena as they are and the knowledge of seeing the multitude and variety of phenomena.

If the Buddha perceived the nature of phenomena without compassion, he would keep this knowledge to himself. So the fifth quality is compassionate love. The Buddha is endowed with perfect compassion quite similar, but stronger than, the love a mother has for her only son. That love implies one wants to free the other person from suffering and have him or her be happy. The Buddha has the most perfect form of compassion and this makes him able to help beings.

The Buddha has perfect knowledge and compassion, but these two qualities can't help all beings if a sixth quality is lacking. To remove all suffering and the cause of suffering, one must have the power to do it. The Buddha has this ability to help others free themselves from suffering and the causes of their suffering with compassion and knowledge. With these he can cut through the seeds of suffering and destroy the wall of doubts.

***Summary of the Qualities***

[6] The first quality is uncreated. If something has a beginning, and an intermediate state where it is abiding, and an end when it disintegrates, then it has the three marks of existence of birth, life, and death which are the characteristics of composite things. Buddhahood is not created because it is inherent in the mind of all beings from the beginning. Because it is always present, there is no cessation of Buddhahood. It is there continually helping beings as long as saṃsāra goes on. In the middle there is no actual presence of Buddhahood in the sense it is solid because its essence is voidness and its nature is clarity. It is therefore a union of voidness and clarity.

The Buddha has spontaneous presence because of his peace and possession of the dharmakāya. By nature the Buddha is peaceful because he has no impulse to harm anything. There are also no emotions that are a result of desire that would push a Buddha into acting to create all this effort and all this striving because in Buddhahood all these aspects of striving and concocting thoughts have disappeared and been purified. So the Buddha is peaceful and has the nature of the dharmakāya which is free from all mental efforts and creations. This is why the Buddha is said to be spontaneous and have the spontaneous presence of all the good qualities.

[7] The third quality of Buddhahood is that it is not realized through external conditions. To realize Buddhahood we don't need to depend on anything external. This does not mean that at the beginning of the path, we do not need help to learn how to practice. At the beginning of the path we cannot see this pure essence of

Buddhahood in all beings so we must rely on external sources. At the moment of realization of Buddhahood, however, we cannot rely on anyone or anything else; we must rely on jñāna which is inherently present in the mind. When the impurities masking jñāna have been removed, the strong clarity of this jñāna is present and recognizes itself.

All beings have the essence of Buddhahood, but they don't know it and therefore need help to reach Buddhahood. The perfect knowledge of the Buddha knows how to help them. Besides this knowledge of how to help there is the compassion which sees the agony beings have to go through again and again. This compassion sees the need to help beings reach Buddhahood which is the only way to truly liberate them.

The Buddha has the power to help remove the suffering and all the defilements of beings that are causing the suffering. So the Buddha sees the need to help others, knows how to help them, and has the ability to do so.

need to help beings reach Buddhahood which is the only way to truly liberate them.

The Buddha has the power to help remove the suffering and all the defilements of beings that are causing the suffering. So the Buddha sees the need to help others, knows how to help them, and has the ability to do so.

# CHAPTER 3

## *The Dharma*

The first vajra point is the Buddha who has eight qualities. When Buddhahood is achieved, the Buddha begins spontaneously helping beings reach enlightenment. How does he do this? Does he give them his blessing and they are immediately transported into Buddhahood? This is not the way the Buddha helps beings. He points out the path of enlightenment to them and helps them by teaching the dharma which is the path of enlightenment. This is why the dharma is the second vajra point.

The word "dharma" has two different meanings: The dharma of statements which are all the teachings of the Buddha passed on to his disciples. These also include the explanatory texts (śāstras) which were written by others to explain the Buddha's words. The words of the Buddha are divided into three "baskets" called the Tripiṭaka. The first is the Vinaya teachings which were intended to free one from attachment. The second basket is the sūtras which are intended to free one from aggression. The third is the Abhidharma which are intended to free one from ignorance. All these teachings add up to 84,000 different facets of the teachings.

The dharma of realization is the result of dharma practice so the bodhisattvas can realize within themselves all the qualities that are described in the teachings such as the six *pāramitās*. The word "dharma" is most frequently used to mean "teaching." In the *Uttara Tantra*, however, the meaning of "dharma" refers to the dharma of realization and is used in the sense of something which has the ability to eliminate all defilements and bring about the full fruition of jñāna (the highest and purest form of knowledge and intelligence). The dharma of statements is only an indirect tool to acquire the qualities, whereas all the qualities of purity and realization can be directly attained with the dharma of realization. In tne *Uttara Tantra* the word "dharma" will be used mostly in its ultimate sense of the realization of these qualities.

The dharma of realization has two aspects: the truth of cessation and the truth of the path. The truth of cessation is "total freedom from bondage." The Tibetan word for bondage is *ching wa*, literally meaning "attachment" or "attached." Sometimes this word "bondage" refers to the defilements related just to attachment. But in this text the word "bondage" is used for all obscurations—the defilements of emotions and the obscurations due to dualistic thinking. The truth of cessation is freedom from both these obscurations and one achieves it when one is free from all these defilements. This truth is achieved by the practice of the path to develop jñāna. When this knowledge is born in one, one can reach the truth of cessation.

### *The Qualities of the Dharma*

[9] The truth of cessation has three qualities, the truth of the path has three qualities and with these two truths, the dharma of realization has eight qualities.

The text first describes dharma in the salutation. It says, "I bow down to the sun of the dharma." The dharma is compared to the sun because when the sun rises, the light of the sun dispels all darkness by shining everywhere spontaneously. Likewise, when one has a direct realization of the dharma, all the defilements and obscurations are dispelled completely.

The first three qualities relate to the truth of cessation and the true nature of phenomena. The first quality is inconceivability because phenomena are devoid of solid reality. When one hears this one should not fall into the extreme of nihilism by thinking "if it is void, then nothing at all has any significance" and begin believing that *karma* does not apply so there is no difference between a good and a bad action. To counteract this nihilism, the text states that emptiness (Skt. *shūnyatā*) is not non-existence. On the relative level, whatever appears to us, even though it is an illusion, is there and our actions do have an effect. However, on the absolute level there are the buddha kāyas or the jñāna of the Buddhas. This presence of the Buddha kāyas and the validity of karma on the relative level are understood by the self-cognizant jñāna. On the relative level, everything manifests; but all these phenomena have never had any actual reality because they are by nature void. With an understanding of the emptiness, one can avoid the other danger of believing in solid existence—the belief in realism.

The true nature of everything (1) is not "nonexistence" and (2) it is not "existence." It is not (3) a combination of existence and nonexistence because this is logically impossible. If one had existed in the first place, then one might be able to combine it with nonexistence. But since there is no existence to begin with, then one cannot combine the two because they are not there in the first place. It is not (4) beyond existence and nonexistence. Again this is impossible because existence and nonexistence cannot combine. It is not possible to be something other than existence or non-existence. This argument shows the true nature of everything is free from the reasoning of these *four extremes* and the true nature is free from the complication of our rational thinking.

This true nature is beyond any verbal definition. If one has an object one can define it with words. The very subtle true nature of everything cannot be defined with words. It is said in many texts that the true nature of things is ineffable (impossible to comprehend), it is beyond words, beyond thoughts, beyond definition. How can one then understand it? First one must gain indirect knowledge of it with logical thinking. Once one has this indirect knowledge of it, then one meditates to obtain a direct understanding of it. This direct understanding comes from the self-cognizant aspect of one's intelligence. All phenomena are devoid of any substantial reality and this emptiness is not just an empty space. If it were an empty space, then it would be a blankness. The emptiness of the mind, in contrast, is the *dharmadhātu* which is the space of the true nature of things and has a very vivid clarity. Within this clarity is the possibility for everything to manifest. This possibility of manifestation can have the quality of purity or impurity. When there is impurity, the manifestation will take illusory forms. When the purity is undisturbed, the manifestation will appear in pure forms and pure lands of the Buddha. So the true nature of phenomena is the essence of emptiness and the nature is clarity. This nature is known by self-cognizant jñāna. When the jñāna knows itself, it knows that nature. Therefore the text says this essence of Buddhahood "is neither existence nor nonexistence."

Now follows a word, "peace," which means total pacification of all karma and all defilements. Even though in the text there is only one word, "peace," this word "peace" points to the two other qualities of the truth of cessation. The second quality is nonduality and the third is freedom from concept. Everything that comes before the word "peace" refers to the quality of inconceivability.

The second quality is stainlessness or purity. There are two kinds of obscurations to be purified on the practice of the path: the emotional aspect of the defilements and the obscurations of dualistic knowledge. Once all the obscurations are removed, the sun of jñāna which is inherently present in the mind can now shine through in all its brilliance. The word "brilliant" refers to the light of jñāna and points out the second quality of clarity. Once the obscurations have been removed, there is total clarity of knowledge because the sun of jñāna has been freed of the clouds.

The third quality is bringing a remedy to all the ailments of the defilements which were obscured by attachment, aggression, and ignorance. When the sun of jñāna has been liberated from its clouds, it dispels all the negativity and remedies it. This is why the truth of the path is compared to the sun in the phrase, "I bow down to the sun of dharma." The sun free from clouds is pure and its brilliance sheds its light everywhere and its qualities remedy darkness. Now in more detail:

[10] The truth of cessation is represented by the achievement of realizing the truth of phenomena. This true nature has the quality of being inconceivable. "Inconceivable" means that the nature of things being beyond the four conceptual extremes is neither existent or nonexistent nor a combination of these two nor beyond these two. It is "inconceivable" in terms of using words.

The second quality is nonduality which means freedom from the impurities of karma and defilements. Karma literally means "action" and refers to all good and bad actions a person does. These actions are always tainted by defilements and dualistic thought. Even when we perform good actions, these actions are still tainted in some subtle sense (such as wanting something in return for the good action) and therefore are still a cause for rebirth. If we perform good actions, they will produce good results and lead to a higher rebirth in saṃsāra. But still they will result in rebirth in saṃsāra. The defilements are the root of ego and the belief in the existence of the self. If there is still the presence of karma and defilements, then there is still saṃsāra. The dharma is free from both karma and defilements and therefore it is called nondual.

The third quality of the truth of cessation is non-conceptual or being totally free from concepts and thoughts. Whenever there are thoughts, there is the danger of incorrect thoughts which are thoughts contradicting the actual nature of things. These incorrect thoughts generate negative actions and defilements and with these one ends up living in saṃsāra. These concepts then are the root of saṃsāra. The truth of cessation doesn't have any of these thoughts which will give rise to saṃsāra.

The quality of stainlessness means free from the stains of defilements and dualistic knowledge. The dharma of the truth of the path is free from these impurities. Even though they may appear, these impurities are only fleeting and not really part of the dharma. The dharma by nature has never been soiled or polluted by these impurities. It is similar to pure gold which might sometimes be tarnished, but that tarnish is not an inherent part of the gold. The tarnish is only a temporary condition that can be eliminated. Similarly, there may be clouds in the sky, but clouds are not an inherent part of the nature of the sky; they are just accidents passing through the sky. In the same way, the impurities of karma, defilements and dualistic knowledge, are just fleeting phenomena happening in the mind and not an integral part of dharma.

When the truth of the path has been completely realized, there is a brilliance which lights up all the appearances of relative reality very clearly. One can also see the true nature of phenomena at the same time with this clarity. One sees phenomena in the relative aspect and the ultimate aspect. When the truth of the path has been achieved, it is like a light that lights up both the relative and absolute aspect of phenomena.

The realization of the qualities of purity and clarity eliminate the defilements of the three poisons: attachment, aggression, and ignorance. Dharma has the intrinsic characteristics of freedom from the causes of bondage. Freedom from bondage relates to the truth of cessation.

Bondage is all the emotional negativities, the obscurations of dualistic knowledge, and the subconscious traces that remain after the coarser impurities have been removed. These obscurations bind one to saṃsāra and these defilements do not disappear by themselves, so one must apply a remedy to the obscurations.

If one practices the path, beginning with the path of accumulation, the path of junction, etc., eventually one attains Buddhahood. The truth of the path frees one from bondage and when bondage has disappeared, one has reached the truth of cessation. So the dharma can be said to be that which has the qualities of the truth of cessation and the truth of the path.

Dharma has two aspects—the dharma of teaching and the dharma of realization. When one takes refuge, one must realize there are two aspects of refuge—refuge as a causal condition leading one to enlightenment and refuge as the result after one has achieved enlightenment. The refuge of cause is taken at the very beginning of the path as ordinary beings by taking refuge in the Buddha, the dharma, and the saṅgha. At this point one does not know the path that leads to Buddhahood and therefore one needs to rely on the Buddha who shows the path as guide. One takes refuge in the dharma as the teachings of the Buddha and one takes refuge in the saṅgha as companions on the path. As an ordinary being one takes refuge in the Buddha who is outside oneself, the dharma that's not one's personal realization, and the saṅgha composed of beings with their own realization. So in the beginning one takes refuge in things realized by other beings and one studies the *Tripiṭaka* as the dharma.

In the *Uttara Tantra*, on the other hand, refuge is in the context of the fruition refuge. One first takes refuge in the three jewels as the cause for one's future enlightenment. When one takes refuge in the saṅgha, one becomes part of the saṅgha. Next on the path if one practices and eliminates the obscurations and impurities. The true qualities of dharma become evident. Then the dharma aspect becomes realized and when one takes refuge in the dharma, it is not external but is internalized. Eventually one becomes a Buddha and does not rely on anything external any more and one becomes one's own refuge. At the fruition level one takes refuge in the dharma of realization rather than in the dharma as a teaching and becomes the realized saṅgha. The *Uttara Tantra* refers to the truth of the path which leads to the truth of cessation and dharma as realization.

### *How the Qualities are Connected to the Truths*

[11] The truth of cessation is freedom from bondage when there is nothing more to relinquish and the truth of the path frees one from bondage. The truth of cessation has qualities of inconceivability, nonduality, and nonconceptuality. The truth of path has the qualities of purity, clarity, and remedy. So the six qualities are contained in the two truths.

### *How the Qualities are Connected to the Salutation*

[12] Asaṅga in the *Uttara Tantra* goes through the qualities three times to make sure they are understood. First, he gives it in the salutation, then he gives it in detail in the second point and then he connects the various qualities with the praise in the third part. In the fourth point, the truth of cessation is presented as inconceivable because it is beyond the grasp of intellect: when one thinks about it, one cannot say it is like this or that or give it a color or definition. Secondly, it is beyond the grasp of speech: it cannot be expressed, it cannot be described in words; one cannot say it is like this or like that. Thirdly, it is inconceivable because it cannot be grasped by the understanding of an ordinary person. In the salutation to the dharma it states that the truth of cessation is self-cognizant and known only to the deeply realized. When one is working on the path, one learns about this truth, then one reflects on it, then one meditates on it. When all impurities have been removed through meditation, one will reach the state of realized ones, the level of the bodhisattvas, when one sees the true nature of phenomena directly without any distortion. Then one will know the truth of cessation directly because the truth of cessation cannot be known by an ordinary mind.

The second quality of peace is inherent in the true nature of phenomena which are endowed with twofold purity. This peace is there because all forms of suffering have been removed because karma and defilements have been relinquished. So first "peace" means suffering has been pacified. Secondly, it is peace because it is completely free from anything rough and coarse or harsh. Thirdly, it is peace because it is nondual or nonconceptual being free from the coarseness of thoughts.

With the three qualities of the truth of the path, purity is a natural feature of the realization because the twofold obscurations have been removed. There is not only purity, but there is also clarity. Once there is purity and clarity, there is the power to remedy the three poisons. In the salutation this is explained in the example of the sun. The sun is by nature very pure, and because of this purity, it dispels all forms of darkness. In the same way, realization of the truth of the path eliminates obscurations, defilements, and dualistic knowledge and brings about the recognition of the natural purity of the nature of phenomena.

# CHAPTER 4

## *The Saṅgha*

In the *Uttara Tantra* the saṅgha is the realized saṅgha, the mahāyāna saṅgha. The Tibetan word for "saṅgha" is *gendun*. The first syllable *ge* means "virtue" and the second *dun* means "aspiration" so *gendun* are those aspiring to virtue. There are two types of saṅgha—that of ordinary beings and that of realized beings. Ordinary beings haven't reached a state of realization and don't have a direct understanding of the truth because they are still subject to the defilements. However, they have strong aspirations to do what is good. The saṅgha of ordinary beings is made up of lay people and ordained people. It is possible to follow the Buddhist path without being ordained but by taking refuge and taking any of the levels of the precepts. At the refuge ceremony one takes refuge in the three jewels which represents ordinary refuge but is also taken by the realized saṅgha. In this refuge ceremony there is no distinction among those who take refuge and the saṅgha is made up of friends and companions who help us on the path and make sure we don't go astray. But the *Uttara Tantra* describes fruition refuge which is the refuge we are trying to achieve ultimately. In this fruition refuge we are trying to go beyond the state of ordinary beings which on the mahāyāna path means achieving Buddhahood and the saṅgha is called the realized saṅgha.

***Definition of the Saṅgha in the Salutation***

[13] The outline of this chapter will be similar to the chapter on the Buddha because it also has three divisions: a definition of the nature of the saṅgha in the salutation, the identification of the qualities in the saṅgha, and a description of the six qualities mentioned in the salutation. The salutation begins, "I bow down..." to the realized saṅgha who possess these qualities by one who is trying to follow their example to reach enlightenment. These qualities are two-fold—the qualities of knowledge and the qualities of purity. The qualities of knowledge make it possible for the realized saṅgha to see the nature of all phenomena just as it is. The qualities of purity allow one to be free of all impurities and obscurations. There are three aspects of this knowledge: the knowledge of how-it-is, the knowledge of variety, and the inner knowledge of jñāna which perceives the presence of buddha potential in all beings. From these three kinds of knowledge come three aspects of freedom: freedom from emotional defilements; freedom from the hindrances of dualistic thinking which blocks the vision of the true nature of phenomena, and the freedom from lower motivation that leads to striving for happiness for just oneself.

[14] The first aspect of knowledge is the jñāna of how-it-is. From the beginning of time the nature of mind has been empty and clear. Emptiness has been emphasized in the Madhyamaka teachings. But in the teachings on meditation, particularly the mahāmudrā, emptiness is considered just one aspect of the nature of the mind with the other aspect being clarity. The real nature of the mind then is a combination of emptiness and clarity. The

defilements of attachment, aggression, and ignorance might or might not be present, but they are not an inherent part of the mind. The defilements are more like mistakes or delusions. The jñāna of how-it-is perceives the true nature of the mind, the one with emptiness and clarity which is described in the next verse.

The second aspect of knowledge, the jñāna of variety, appears once one has the knowledge of the ultimate nature of phenomena and there is such great clarity that one can see the actual nature of beings—each and every being just as he or she is. Through the jñāna of variety of phenomena one sees the true nature of beings as being the ultimate "no-self." One discovers that the self does not exist in reality and this is the actual nature of all beings.

The third aspect of the realized saṅgha is the pure vision gained through the inner jñāna and thus "they know the all-pervasive presence of perfect Buddhahood in each and every one of them." Through this aspect of knowledge individuals see the essence of Buddhahood in themselves and all the other beings. This essence is like the germ of the jñāna of the Buddha and that seed is in the mind of all beings. At the stage of ordinary beings, this essence of Buddhahood does not manifest. At the stage of bodhisattvas, this essence manifests to some extent. Only when one has achieved enlightenment can this essence fully manifest into Buddhahood. The difference between these three types of beings is not one of nature because the essence of the Buddha is the same in all beings. So this is what is "seen though inner jñāna."

In the salutation it says that the realized saṅgha are unobscured in intelligence and this word "unobscured" refers to the three qualities of freedom. The first freedom is from emotional obscurations—attachment, aggression, or ignorance. The second freedom is from the obscuration of dualistic thinking. Dualistic thinking is to think in terms of subject and object and to believe everything is substantial. The third freedom is from a combination of the previous two obscurations which creates the mistake of wanting to find happiness just for oneself such as the *śrāvakas* or *pratyekabuddhas* do. In summary, through jñāna the realized saṅgha possesses three types of knowledge so they can see the ultimate purity of the nature of all beings. These six qualities are summarized in Table 1.

In the third chapter on the Buddha, the ultimate dharmakāya was discussed without discussing the sambhogakāya and nirmāṇakāya. In the chapter on the dharma the scriptural dharma and dharma of realization were discussed and the realization dharma was emphasized. In the discussion of the saṅgha, the ordinary and the realized saṅgha were discussed with the emphasis on the realized saṅgha. So in these three chapters the approach has emphasized the ultimate, highest form of the Buddha, the dharma, and the saṅgha.

### *Six Qualities of the Saṅgha*

[15] The knowledge of how-it-is in its fullest degree is only achieved with Buddhahood. When one is on the path of the bodhisattva, this knowledge is present to a varying degree. With knowledge of how-it-is one does not perceive the relative aspect, the illusory appearance of phenomena, but sees it just as it is without any distortion. For example, if one sees a rope in the dark, one might mistake it for a snake. The knowledge of how-it-is wouldn't see the rope

as a snake because the nature of how-it-is does not see the illusory appearances of saṃsāra. This knowledge experiences the actual nature of phenomena which is the nature of the dharmadhātu, the original nature. This is the nature and function of this knowledge of how-it-is.

[16] The jñāna of variety of phenomena is to see what there is in many aspects, not just 10 things or 100 things, but to see everything in its great diversity. The knowledge of how-it-is pertains to absolute truth, the knowledge of variety pertains to the relative truth. So with the knowledge of variety one sees everything: one sees the number of beings, one sees the motivations of the beings, and one sees all the various appearances of existence. One also sees the characteristics of objects such as their colors, form, etc., but there's no confusion in seeing them, they are each seen very distinctly. Realized beings perceive the relative reality of all appearances and their perception is not divorced from the knowledge of how-it-is. When one sees relative phenomena, one does not get caught up in confusion and illusion. So even though realized beings can see the relative, at the same time they know the ultimate level, which means they cannot go back to seeing illusions.

[17] The third quality of the perception of inner jñāna is very intimately connected to the knowledge of how-it-is and the knowledge of variety. It is connected with the knowledge of how-it-is because jñāna perceives the true, absolute nature of phenomena; the "thatness of suchness." It doesn't see phenomena as totally empty but being indivisible from all the qualities of Buddhahood. This perception is also connected with the knowledge of variety by perceiving all beings as possessing the essence of Buddhahood. The word "inner" in "inner jñāna" (Tib.

*nang gi yeshe*); refers to the fact that it belongs to the true nature of the mind. "Jñāna" (Tib. *yeshe*) refers to the fact that of the two aspects of phenomena, emptiness and clarity, with jñāna being the clarity aspect. This jñāna has the capacity to develop fully into all the qualities of freedom and maturity of a Buddha and knows that the inner jñāna present in all beings.

[18] Perception with the three aspects of knowledge is absolutely pure and this relates to the three qualities of purity. The realized ones are free from the three types of obscurations of attachment, aggression, or ignorance. If they had these they would act in a negative way causing them to be trapped in saṃsāra and the three aspects of pure knowledge would not arise. In the case of śrāvakas, for example, who are free of the first obscuration of emotions the realized saṅgha is most important.

[19] There are three reasons for the presentation of the division of three refuges. The first is that there are the three vehicles (Skt. *yānas*) of the hīnayāna, mahāyāna, and vajrayāna. The second reason for the division of three refuges is that there are three types of deeds. There are deeds of making prostrations, offerings, and prayers to the Buddha. Individuals doing these feel the Buddha is really the best of all beings and a model to respect. Others feel that the dharma is really the most important thing because it is the path of liberation and they feel great faith and respect for the teachings. The third category of persons feels the most important point for them is the saṅgha so they will direct most of their deeds towards building the saṅgha.

The third reason for the division of the three refuges is just personal preference: some are more attracted to the

Buddha, some to the dharma, and some to the saṅgha as a refuge.

### *Dharma and Saṅgha are not the Ultimate Refuge*

[20] The only ultimate source of refuge is the Buddha. The dharma and saṅgha are a refuge on the way to Buddhahood, but once one becomes a Buddha there is no longer any need for the props of dharma and saṅgha. Scriptural dharma cannot be an ultimate refuge because upon achieving Buddhahood, one leaves the teachings behind and no longer has any need to practice them. The dharma of realization is not the ultimate refuge either. On the path one goes through different stages of realization and as soon as one reaches one level, then the previous one becomes obsolete. Because the path changes all the time, how could it be an ultimate source of refuge? The truth of cessation cannot be the ultimate source of refuge because once one develops realization, one doesn't have anything to show for it—something tangible; rather one becomes free from what is unwanted. The truth of cessation is eliminating what is unwanted and not acquiring something positive, so it cannot be the ultimate source of refuge.

[21] The saṅgha is not the ultimate source of refuge because it still has fear. The saṅgha has not totally travelled the path and still needs to take refuge in the Buddha and therefore is not beyond all fears.

In the ultimate sense only the Buddha is the true refuge. All suffering and difficulties disappear only when changeless happiness is reached and this occurs only when one becomes a Buddha. Therefore the Buddha is the only real refuge. Does this mean that refuge in the dharma and saṅgha is not very good? No, because dharma and saṅgha are qualities that include the Buddha. The Buddha is the dharmakāya which literally means the "embodiment of dharma." The saṅgha are beings who are working on the path to Buddhahood and go from one level to another until they finally reach complete realization. The qualities of the Buddha are also the ultimate attainment of the saṅgha, so it can be said that in the Buddha all the qualities of the dharma and the saṅgha are present. This is why the Buddha is the ultimate refuge.

***Why They are Called the Three Jewels***

[22] The original Sanskrit word for "jewel" in the three jewels was *ratna* and a literal translation into Tibetan should have been *rinpoche* which means "very precious" or having great value. But the Tibetan translators did not chose a literal translation but preferred another word because when one says something has great value, one is emphasizing its outer quality. The three jewels are so much greater so it was translated it as *kern cho. Kern* means "rare" and *cho* means "supreme" or "most excellent." They chose the word *kern* because the three jewels are most rare and *cho* because they are unsurpassable.

There are six reasons why the Buddha, dharma, and saṅgha are referred to as rare and supreme in Tibetan. First, a jewel is very rare and there aren't many persons who encounter one. Likewise the Buddha, dharma, and saṅgha are quite rare and many persons do not encounter them. Second, jewels are stainless. When one finds a jewel, it is very bright and shiny and not dirty or repulsive. Similarly, the three jewels are very pure because they are totally free from all emotional stains. Third, possessing jewels is to have power. When one possesses a jewel, one has something of great value and by selling it one can obtain financial power which allows one to accomplish many things. Similarly, the three jewels are powerful because they can extinguish all the suffering of beings. Fourth, a jewel is an ornament which makes things more beautiful by its presence. In the same way, the three jewels are ornaments of the world because they bring much goodness to the world because their basic motivation is to benefit other beings with their mere presence. Also the three jewels have such a great sense of self-respect and won't behave incorrectly because they are very careful in their behavior. They have enough respect of others so they will not behave incorrectly towards them. So these beings have a very high and pure quality because of the way they behave. People who practice the path of dharma on the whole will achieve the final realization of the path. So as time goes by there will be more and more beings who reach the highest state and there will be more and more ornaments of the world. The fifth reason is that the three jewels have the quality of excellence. In our world there are many different persons who are supposed to be wonderful because they have achieved fame or success or wealth. But these worldly achievements are not permanent and ultimately are not capable of being beneficial. But the three jewels bring eternal peace and changeless happiness. The sixth reason is the three jewels can bring fruition that is changeless. This is similar to a jewel because it doesn't disintegrate. Once one has reached Buddhahood, there is no possibility of falling back into confusion and suffering.

## *Table 1*

### *Outline of the first Three Vajra Points*

| VAJRA POINT I<br>**The Buddha**<br>*Based on the truth of* | VAJRA POINT II<br>**The Dharma**<br>*Based on the truth of* | VAJRA POINT III<br>**The Saṅgha**<br>*Based on the truth of* |
|---|---|---|
| **Value for Oneself (1**)** | **Value for Oneself (1)** | **Value for Oneself (1)** |
| 1.* Uncreated (2) | 1. Inconceivable (2) | 1. Knowledge of how-it-is (2) |
| 2. Spontaneous presence (3) | 2. Nonduality (3) | 2. Knowledge of manyness (3) |
| 3. No external conditions (4) | 3. Nonconceptuality (4) | 3. Inner jñāna (4) |
| **Value for Others (5)** | **Value for Others (5)** | **Value for Others (5)** |
| 4. Perfect knowledge (6) | 4. Stainlessness (6) | 4. Free from defilements (6) |
| 5. Compassionate love (7) | 5. Brilliance (7) | 5. Free from dualism (7) |
| 6. Power to remedy (8) | 6. Remdial power (8) | 6. Free from lower paths (8) |

* The number in front are for counting the qualities using the 6-quality method of counting.
** the numbers behind are for tor using the 8-quality counting method.

# CHAPTER 5

# An Introduction to Book II: *The Last Four Vajra Points*

The last four vajra points are buddha essence,[4] enlightenment, the buddha qualities, and the buddha activities. Each vajra point will be divided into two parts: a general description and then a more detailed description. This introduction will be a description of these last four vajra points which cannot be understood directly by ordinary beings.

### *The Nature of Each Point*

[23] The nature of *sugatagarbha* or buddha nature is unpolluted suchness which is the true condition of phenomena when it is not distorted by illusion or confusion created by the mind. In the example of mistaking a rope for a snake, if one knows the suchness of the rope, then one doesn't have any fear. Normally, the suchness of everything is distorted by the illusion of saṃsāra, even though the actual nature of suchness of phenomena is emptiness and clarity. So this polluted suchness is similar to buddha nature. If one has a jewel covered with mud and

[4] The fourth vajra point is *sugatagarbha* (Tib. *der sheg nying po*). This will be referred to as "buddha nature" or "essence of Buddhahood" for variety.

one removes the mud, one can see the jewel in its purity. Because the nature of the jewel is pure, one can remove the impurities and it will still retain its purity. In the same way, buddha nature is stainless in that when one removes the emotional and cognitive obscurations, there will be the presence of unpolluted suchness which is Buddhahood. Once all the impurities are removed, the suchness can manifest in all its purity and becomes enlightenment which is the second of the last four vajra qualities. When the suchness has been purified, all the qualities inherent in the suchness can manifest; these are the buddha qualities which are the third of the last four vajra points. The buddha qualities represent total fulfillment for oneself and others. It is fulfillment for oneself because all the causes of suffering, karma, have been removed. This happiness is complete and unchanging because all causes of happiness are present. From the qualities of Buddhahood spring the power to help other beings creating the fourth of the last vajra points, buddha activity. Buddhahood is the supreme way to help all beings and as long as saṃsāra goes on and it will help an infinite number of beings. Buddha activity also doesn't give just temporary relief from suffering, but helps achieve ultimate happiness.

It is said that before we see the three jewels as rare and supreme, we see them as refuge with the Buddha being the ultimate refuge. But where do these refuges come from? They arise from the above four qualities of unpolluted suchness, the qualities of Buddhahood, and the deeds of Buddhahood. Through these qualities one can achieve the three refuges. It is difficult for ordinary persons to understand how these last four vajra points can bring the realization of the three jewels because only Buddhas are capable of seeing this directly.

[24] The Buddha can perceive the last four vajra points and understand them fully. The three jewels are the fruition of the realization of the path. Only the Buddhas can see the causal ground because they are endowed with pure vision of how-it-is and variety of all phenomena. Therefore buddha nature, enlightenment, buddha qualities, and buddha activities are inconceivable to ordinary beings.

[25] There are four reasons why the four vajra points are inconceivable to ordinary beings. First, the essence of enlightenment is inconceivable because it is pure but is also accompanied by defilements. The essence of enlightenment is perfectly and naturally pure from the very beginning having never known any stain. Yet it is accompanied by defilements and this sounds like a paradox. Thinking about suchness being present with defilements in the mind is quite inconceivable to ordinary beings. If one tries to meditate on it, one can't experience it directly; therefore it is perceived only by the Buddhas. Second, enlightenment is inconceivable to ordinary beings because enlightenment is completely free from defilements, yet has to be purified. Buddha nature is completely pure and through gradual purification buddha nature manifests in its full purity (enlightenment). So there is a logical contradiction between the original purity and the need to purify it through practice. Third, the buddha qualities are inconceivable because they are inseparable from buddha nature. From the beginning all the qualities of Buddhahood are present in buddha nature, but one achieves all these qualities only when one reaches Buddhahood. Fourth, buddha activity is inconceivable because it is both spontaneous and nonconceptual. Buddha activity occurs without effort on the part of the Buddha.

This activity responds to what people need, yet the Buddha doesn't need to think, "I must do this for this person." Yet all the time the activity is happening exactly in the way needed for each and every being.

[26] The reasons that these vajra points are inconceivable is they appear to be paradoxes. But with closer examination there is no real contradiction. First, buddha nature is perfectly pure from the viewpoint of its nature or essence. The impurities, the defilements, are only the fruition of a mistaken view and therefore has nothing to do with the actual nature of buddha nature. Second, the defilements can be removed because they are not an inherent part of enlightenment, so they can not pollute its nature. If one looks at the qualities there is no real contradiction either because from the viewpoint of the actual nature these qualities have always been inseparable and present in the essence of Buddhahood. But when covered up by impurities, they cannot display their presence in action. When impurities are removed, the qualities function as they ought to do. It's similar to what happens when the sun is covered by clouds. When the sun is covered by clouds, the sunlight cannot manifest; however the light itself has not been changed. In the same way, when the qualities of enlightenment are covered up by impurities or not. When they're covered up by impurities, these qualities do not manifest. The fourth point of activity is also not a contradiction. Buddha activity is spontaneous, effortless, and nonconceptual. It is the result of all the previous wishes and resolutions and prayers made by the Buddhas when they were on the path to enlightenment. From the strong impetus of previous practice all this activity can arise spontaneously and without any conceptualization.

### *The Realization of these Vajra Points*

The essence of Buddhahood is actual realization. The attributes that spring from this realization are the qualities that bring about realization to other beings. Buddha nature constitutes the causal conditions and the other three vajra points constitute a result that : akes it possible to purify other beings.

AN INTRODUCTION TO BOOK TWO 53

*The Realization of these Vajra Points*

The essence of Buddhahood is actual realization. The attributes that spring from this realization are the qualities that bring about realization to other beings. Buddha nature constitutes the causal conditions and the other three vajra points constitute a result that : akes it possible to purify other beings.

# CHAPTER 6

# Buddha Nature:
## *The Ten Aspects*

This chapter is divided into four parts. The first part is a summary of the meaning of the essence of Buddhahood. The second is a more detailed explanation. The third part illustrates through examples how one can purify buddha nature and the fourth part gives the purpose for teaching about buddha nature.

### *What is Buddha Nature?*

The Buddha taught three turnings of the wheel of dharma. In the first turning the Buddha taught the four noble truths concerning mostly the relative level of reality. We perceive the nature of suffering which is the first noble truth. The origin of this suffering is to be found in all our previous actions and emotional obscurations. The third noble truth of cessation of suffering appears when one eliminates these two causes of suffering. Finally, in order to realize the truth of cessation one has to enter the proper path which is the truth of the path. The Buddha then showed how one has to progress along five different levels of the path before reaching complete enlightenment. In the second turning the Buddha taught about the ultimate nature of phenomena. He said that all phenomena are empty by nature. In the third turning the Buddha went further by showing that this emptiness of phenomena does not mean simple absence of things. When beings are in the impure phase, they still possess the essence of Buddhahood. When they reach Buddhahood, there's the presence of the twofold jñāna of the how-it-is and variety of phenomena. So the third turning goes beyond the meaning of the first two turnings.

[27] The *Uttara Tantra* relates to the third turning because it is concerned with the presence of buddha nature in all beings. There are three reasons for buddha nature being present in all beings. First, the dharmakāya of the Buddha pervades all phenomena and can give rise to any phenomena so it is present everywhere. Second, the suchness or the actual nature of nirvāṇa and samsāric phenomena is undifferentiated so there's no "good suchness" which relates to nirvāṇa and no "bad suchness" which relates to samsāra. There is only one suchness of all phenomena. Third, all beings possess the foundation for buddha nature and when purified it can develop into full Buddhahood.

### *Ten Qualities of Buddha Nature*

[29] There are ten different aspects from which one can approach the essence of Buddhahood. These are nature, cause, result, influence, endowments, approach, the various phases, all-pervasiveness, unalterability, and inseparability of its qualities. These are listed in Table 2 .

### *1. Nature*

[30] The nature of buddha nature is explained by means of three examples of a jewel, the sky, and water. The

significance of these examples will be given later. The dharmakāya is like a jewel because it is totally free from any impurities. It is like the sky when there are no clouds present because the sky by nature is free from clouds. It is like water because water is naturally very pure and the impurities found in water are not part of the nature of the water. In the same way, buddha nature is perfectly pure.

There are four different ways to make buddha nature manifest. First, one must aspire to the dharma because with no aspiration obviously one will not practice it. The second way is to let the essence of buddha nature shine in its clarity and this is accomplished with intelligence (prajñā). The third way is by *samādhi* (meditation) and the fourth is compassion. Without study one will not reflect on buddha nature or without meditation one will not be able to go through the process that makes buddha nature manifest. In more detail:

[31] In the example of the jewel, buddha nature possesses tremendous power because it has the power to achieve ultimate happiness Buddhahood, which is of greatest value for all beings. So it is extremely precious and powerful and is compared to a jewel because a jewel has the power to dispel poverty.

The essence of Buddhahood is compared to the sky because the sky never changes. The earth is constantly changing, but the sky even over periods of thousands of years never turns into anything different. In the same way, the suchness of all phenomena is unchanging and there is no alteration of its nature.

The essence of Buddhahood is compared to water because water has a wet and flowing quality which allows it to go everywhere. By its mere presence everything can grow. Buddha nature also possesses a moistening quality, the lubricating quality of compassion.

So buddha nature has the moistening quality of compassion, the unchanging quality of space, and the power of a jewel.

### *2. Cause*

[32] In our present condition of ordinary beings the essence of Buddhahood has not manifested because we encounter the four unfavorable obstacles of Buddhahood. The first obstacle is having hostility or a natural dislike for the dharma. One may wish not to have anything to do with dharma and not want to practice. Obviously, one will never enter the dharma with this kind of attitude. Even without hostility towards the dharma, there may be no confidence in the value of the teaching so there is the feeling that everything taught is useless. The second obstacle is the strong belief in the reality of self. Even if one is interested in the dharma and wishes to practice, if one has a very solid belief in ego, one will encounter an obstacle in the manifestation of buddha nature because a belief in self is contradictory to the understanding of attaining Buddhahood and is also the root of all negativity. To have the essence of Buddhahood manifest; one has to remove the two types of emotional and cognitive obscurations. But with a very strong belief in a self then, one cannot begin to remove these obscurations. The third obstacle is the fear of suffering in samsāra because this fear will prevent one from entering the mahāyāna path. We are striving to eliminate suffering, but there has to be an understanding of the void nature of this suffering at the same time. If one

can understand that suffering is void, then one doesn't fear this suffering and is able to help all beings attain freedom from suffering. The fourth obstacle is the lack of an inclination to help other beings. This occurs when one feels one's own problems are enough and so one is not really interested in what happens to others. Someone with this attitude who practices is going to reach the higher states of rebirth in samsāra and a form of liberation such as that of the *arhats*, but it will not be complete liberation of buddha nature manifesting into Buddhahood.

[33] Each obstacle has a type of person attached to it. The first obstacle is associated with persons hostile to the dharma. The second obstacle can be found in many religions. Some religions include a need to eliminate a belief in a self, but many do not even consider this quality; the self is just considered normal and does not have to be relinquished. The Buddhist term for people holding this belief in self is *tīrthika*. Tīrthikas are people who are fairly close to the dharma in that they are religious, but the religious belief is not powerful enough to manifest the essence of Buddhahood because they still believe in the presence of a self. The third obstacle is present in the śrāvakas who are individuals who want to find liberation only for themselves because they are afraid of suffering. The fourth obstacle is found in pratyekabuddhas.

These four obstacles can be removed by their opposite qualities. Aspiration for the dharma will eliminate hostility towards the dharma. Great prajñā will eliminate belief in self. The best form of meditation, samādhi, will eliminate the fear of samsāra. Compassion will eliminate the lack of interest in the sufferings of other beings.

In the *Uttara Tantra* the main emphasis is on view. There is, of course, mention of how to practice, but the view is the main point of the text. The text shows quite clearly the actual nature of phenomena and two aspects emerge—the empty aspect and the clarity aspect. The empty aspect is the spacious, unreal aspect. The clarity aspect is the intelligence, the vivid understanding. In this text these two aspects are shown to be the inseparable union of emptiness and clarity and that is buddha nature.

To summarize, buddha potential can be examined from its innate aspect and the aspect developed through practice. Through practice and the presence of certain qualities, buddha nature can manifest. But in trying to make it manifest one meets four kinds of obstacles. If these four obstacles can be overcome with the help of the four favorable conditions, then one can work towards Buddhahood and little by little approach the state of the son of a Buddha—a bodhisattva.

[34] The birth of a bodhisattva can, for example, be compared to the birth of a child. First there is aspiration for the dharma, not just dharma in general, but the highest form of dharma, the mahāyāna. Aspiration for the dharma creates all of the qualities needed on the path and will eventually lead to Buddhahood. This is compared to the semen of the father which can give birth to a child. This seed needs a mother so once one aspires to the dharma, one will want to practice and develop the quality of understanding of non-self, and the understanding of the true nature of phenomena. This quality of prajñā is compared to the mother because the semen needs a special environment for it to develop and this is the womb of the mother. The womb represents meditation. If there is some degree of understanding of non-self and the nature of phenomena, this understanding will grow more and more.

This is like the embryo of a child that needs to develop in the favorable environment of the womb until the body is fully complete with all its limbs and so on. Similarly, prajñā needs the favorable environment of meditation to reach full development. The fourth quality of compassion is compared to a nursemaid. When the baby is born, he still needs much care. With proper care and attention, the baby's body will grow and his intelligence will develop and eventually he will be an adult. The nursemaid is compassion because compassion makes the qualities of prajñā and meditation grow. With compassion for beings, one's understanding grows and one's meditation improves. So this example shows that if one has the four qualities of aspiration, prajñā, meditation, and compassion one can become a son of the Buddha and truly work on the path of enlightenment.

The meditation referred to here is mostly tranquility meditation (śamatha). It is constantly connected to the intelligent side of prajñā and with the compassionate side of caring for beings. Without these two qualities meditation is devoid of the understanding of non-self and will not be able to cut the root of saṃsāra and will create karma which brings about rebirth in a form or formless realm.

### 3. Fruition

The third quality is the fruition that occurs when buddha nature has completely manifested. The fourth quality is the influence of buddha nature that occurs once buddha nature has completely manifested. These two points are dealt with together because they are similar in that fruition is the ultimate goal and influence is the immediate goal.

[35] The fruition of buddha nature has the transcendental qualities of purity, identity, happiness, and permanence. Complete purity is achieved when Buddhahood is achieved. When one is beyond self and non-self, one achieves the transcendental quality of identity. There is also the quality of transcendental happiness and permanence at the time of fruition. The text states that the function of buddha nature is "revulsion for suffering" and longing for peace. Buddha nature makes us recognize the suffering of our existence. When we have recognized this, we develop a longing to go beyond suffering. This aspiration is present in all beings, being hazy in some persons and very clear in others. The degree of clarity of buddha nature depends on our circumstances. If the right conditions occur, then individuals will meet a teacher and be able to follow the path. Those who have not encountered these external conditions and still have the wish to eliminate suffering will not know that there is a path to liberation. So the influence of buddha nature is to make individuals want to eliminate suffering and find happiness.

[36] There are four things that contradict these conditions of the dharmakāya. They are impurity, suffering, impermanence, and absence of true transcendent identity. When one dwells in saṃsāra, one interprets things incorrectly; one believes what is impure as is pure, one believes what is selfless is possesses a self, one believes something permanent is impermanent, and one believes that suffering is happiness. These are the features of our saṃsāric illusion; we perceive everything as opposite to what it really is. In the hīnayāna teachings the Buddha taught what we believe is pure is not; that the belief in self

is mistaken; that phenomena are devoid of any self-entity; that we believe is happiness is really suffering and misery; what we take for permanent is actually impermanent. In the relative aspect of reality saṃsāra is impure, selfless, suffering, and impermanent. From the ultimate level of reality, however, these four aspects of saṃsāra are no longer relevant. The ultimate reality transcends the four aspects and their opposites and goes beyond pure and impure, non-self and self, etc.

[37] The quality of transcendental purity is beyond pure and impure. It is not the concept of purity of ordinary beings, nor is it free from the impurities as understood by śrāvakas and pratyekabuddhas; it is a purity beyond these notions. There are two aspects to this purity: the purity of true nature and the purity from incidental impurities. The purity of buddha nature is extremely pure and complete; it is masked just by impurities. It is transcendental purity because when these fleeting purities have been removed, the purity is complete.

The second quality is the transcendental quality of identity. The belief in self of ordinary beings has two different aspects—innate belief in self and the habit of thinking of self as "I." Innate belief in self occurs when we are born because no one needs to teach us that we are "I;" we just automatically think of ourselves as "I." This belief in a self is also found in some religions which believe in the existence of the self which has to be liberated.

In contrast, the belief in non-self is developed by those who practice the hīnayāna and the general aspect of the mahāyāna. What is important to understand is that both the belief in a self and a belief in non-self are just mental concepts and have no actual reality. Transcendental identity corresponds to the complete pacification and disappearance of all illusory fabrications of the idea of a self or non-self.

[38] The third quality is the transcendental quality of happiness. When one is born in saṁsāra, one is subjected to different types of suffering—all-pervading suffering and the suffering of change. But one is not aware of the real suffering in conditioned existence, so one believes that to achieve happiness is to remain lost in saṃsāra.

On the hīnayāna path one learns that the actual nature of saṃsāra is suffering. So one meditates on this and develops a conviction that this is true and practices abandoning the causes of suffering. But in the special aspect of the mahāyāna teachings, it is taught that the view of suffering and happiness of saṃsāra are illusory and that the actual nature of phenomena is beyond both these concepts. One learns that suffering is only a mental creation of the five aggregates, being produced by the very fine mental imprints on the mind created by ignorance. The ultimate nature is beyond both the idea of suffering and the idea of happiness and this is transcendental happiness.

The fourth quality is transcendental permanence. When one is an ordinary person lost in saṃsāra, one believes all things are lasting, permanent, even though all conditioned things are actually impermanent. So the belief in permanence is an illusion. In the hīnayāna practice the teachings reverse the idea of permanence replacing it with the concept of impermanence. But in the ultimate sense, both of these ideas and concepts have no actual reality. The actual nature of things is beyond the ideas of permanence and impermanence; it is transcendental permanence because the whole of saṃsāra and nirvāṇa is identical and the qualities inherent in nirvāṇa are already present in saṃsāra. This permanence should be understood in terms of no change because everything is identical.

There are four transcendental qualities: purity, identity, happiness, and permanence. Considering these in the light of the hīnayāna or the general mahāyāna can be extremely surprising because these transcendental qualities seem to contradict the teachings of the Buddha. But these four transcendental qualities are given in terms of the ultimate nature of phenomena which is beyond the limiting extremes of suffering and happiness, of permanence and impermanence, of self and non-self, and purity and impurity.

[39] Once we have achieved these four transcendental qualities, we are free from the extremes of saṃsāra and nirvāṇa and will not fall back into saṃsāra or enter into the one-sided nirvāṇa of liberation for ourselves. So this fruition is the achievement of liberation of the two extremes prajñā preventing us from falling into saṃsāra and compassion preventing us from liberating just ourselves. There are two aspects to a belief in a self—the personal and the phenomenal self-entity. Through prajñā, the highest form of spiritual intelligence, we can cut the root of this misconception and become free of emotional and cognitive obscurations as well as all the fine mental imprints. With compassion we see beyond our own personal interest and satisfaction. In the root text it says those with compassionate love will "cut through all self-cherishing" because they cherish all beings. Cherishing means not to drop them without any concerns, but to really help them.

### *4. The Function of Buddha Nature*

[40] The influence or function of buddha nature is covered in two points. The first point discusses what would happen if buddha nature were not present in all beings. If beings didn't have buddha nature, they wouldn't feel weariness of suffering and wouldn't therefore want to go beyond suffering (nirvāṇa). One can see that non-sentient objects such as trees or stones don't have buddha nature; consequently they don't have any wish to achieve Buddhahood. So this is what would be missing if buddha nature weren't there.

[41] Secondly, saṃsāra will inherently bring much pain and difficulties. Of course, there will be some happiness and satisfaction, but this happiness is likely to change and become pain. So when we are in saṃsāra, we are likely to experience pain. By possessing buddha nature, we are able to see that worldly existence brings suffering and can conceive of nirvāṇa. So we can aspire to go beyond the suffering of conditioned existence. If one didn't have this seed of Buddhahood, it would be impossible to perceive these aspects and strive for nirvāṇa.

### *5. Endowments of Buddha Nature*

[42] The fifth point is endowments or literally possessing the qualities of buddha nature at the moment of fruition. Buddha nature can be compared to the ocean because the ocean contains many precious things. In the same way, buddha nature has the potential for achieving Buddhahood because it already has all the various qualities of Buddhahood. These qualities are the qualities of the

body of the Buddha and the qualities required on the path to Buddhahood had such as faith, courage, prajñā, and so on. These various qualities are also inseparable and this is demonstrated in a comparison of a butter lamp. In more detail:

[43] Buddha nature possesses three seeds—the seeds of the dharmakāya, the seeds of jñāna, and the seeds of compassion. The completely pure dhamakāya of the Buddhas is the first seed of aspiration. Buddha nature can arise only in those who have the aspiration to achieve enlightenment.

The second seed for realizing the jñāna of the Victorious Ones (the Buddhas) is prajñā. The ground from which prajñā develops is meditation. In ordinary beings prajñā is fairly weak and with cultivation it becomes greater and greater until it blossoms into the full jñāna of the Buddhas. Fully developed this jñāna becomes the jñāna of how-it-is and the jñāna of variety.

The third seed is the great compassion of the Buddhas. The Buddhas have perfect compassion which is free from any conceptual reference point and the fruition of this seed leads to enlightenment. So within buddha nature is contained all the seeds of the future qualities of the Buddhas.

In comparing the endowments of buddha nature with an ocean, the vastness of the ocean is compared to the aspiration for enlightenment. The qualities of prajñā and meditation are compared to the jewels in the ocean. Buddha nature contains these two qualities which are very precious because they give rise to the twofold jñāna of the Buddhas. To show that prajñā and meditation are not just dry qualities, the wetness of the ocean is compared to a the "wet" quality of compassion.

[44] In the second example, the qualities of buddha nature at the time of fruition are compared to a butter lamp. Buddha nature is completely stainless, totally pure in nature even though some fleeting impurities are covering it temporarily. The essence of Buddhahood at fruition has the qualities of clear cognition (Tib. *ngon she*), jñāna, and freedom from impurities. The quality of clear cognition has five powers relating to the variety of phenomena. The first power of cognition is "divine vision" which is the ability to see extremely distant and small things. The second power is the "divine ear" which is the ability to hear very distant and very soft sounds. The third power is the "knowledge of the mind of others" which is clairvoyance or exactly knowing the thoughts of others. The fourth power is "knowledge of the past" which is being able to see things going back thousands of years. Fifth is the power of "miraculous transformation of one's body." All of these powers of clear cognition relate to Buddha's jñāna.

The second quality of jñāna refers to the knowledge of how-it-is. It perceives phenomena as merely manifestations, not having any actual reality; so this jñāna is stainless because it isn't polluted by any belief in reality.

The third quality is clarity. There are two aspects of knowledge: knowing the relative and knowing the ultimate. These are always present together; when one knows the variety of phenomena, one knows the true nature of phenomena and one has the third quality of clarity. The parallel between these three qualities is demonstrated with a butter lamp's light, heat, and color. The light can dispel darkness; once darkness is gone one can see everything very clearly. So the brightness of the light is compared to the clear cognition which can see phenomena very clearly.

The stainless jñāna is compared with the heat of the butter lamp because the heat is inseparable from the brightness of the flame. So the stainless jñāna of the Buddha is inseparable from this essence of Buddhahood. The color of the butter lamp refers to the great clarity of the knowledge of the Buddha. This example of the butter lamp shows how that these three qualities of buddha nature are inseparable.

### *6. Manifestation or Approach*

[45] Buddha nature is present in all beings, its essential nature never changes or transforms into anything. Some individuals understand this, some do not, and the teachings describe three types of individuals. First there are ordinary beings who are not yet free of their emotional instability. Then there are more evolved persons, the bodhisattvas. Third there are the perfect Buddhas which can be illustrated by the Tibetan name for "Buddha" which is formed of two syllables *sang gay*. *Sang* means "pure," and *gay* means "perfectly blossomed." So perfect purity represented in the first syllable of *sangay* and perfect knowledge represented in the second syllable. When the qualifier of "perfect" is added one finds that all the qualities of purity and understanding are perfectly complete in the Buddha.

These three types of individuals have three different approaches to buddha essence. The ordinary beings will approach it in a mistaken way, the bodhisattvas will approach it without mistake, and the Buddhas will see it directly. The difference is simply their approach to buddha nature, but the object of their approach, enlightenment, is the same for all of them. In more detail:

[46] Ordinary beings approach buddha nature in a completely incorrect direction. This can be understood in an example of a rope in a dark place that someone mistakes for a snake. If one person sees it is as a snake and another person sees it as only a rope, one of them has a mistaken perception and the other the right perception even though both are looking at the same thing. So it is with buddha nature: ordinary beings see it incorrectly and the bodhisattvas see it correctly. But there is still a third way to see it, the Buddhas see buddha nature just as it is with their direct, clear, extensive, vast, and complete vision. The bodhisattvas, for instance, see it clearly, but do not see it in its entirety. So it is said that the Buddhas see buddha nature completely, just as it is, with the complete absence of conceptual interference.

*7. Phases*

[47] The seventh point describes buddha nature in terms of phases: the impure phase, the slightly impure phase, and the totally pure phase. The impure phase is the stage of ordinary beings in which buddha nature is obscured by the emotional and cognitive obscurations. The mixed phase is purer than the first, but there are still some impurities left. There are two kinds impurities—impurities from insight and impurities from cultivation of this insight.

The bodhisattvas are in the mixed stage and have relinquished impurities of insight which are intellectually created perceptions. Usually one has many concepts about things and generally sees phenomena in a distorted way. The bodhisattvas have eliminated the concepts that obscure the true nature of things, but they haven't dispelled the "innate obscuration" which can only be eliminated by cultivation of this insight. The Buddhas, on the other hand, are in the third stage of having purified all obscurations.

[48] In summary, buddha nature is described in terms of three phases of impure, partially pure, and completely pure. These are similar to the six points of nature, cause, and so on. This impure phase corresponds to ordinary beings; partially pure to bodhisattvas, and completely pure to *tathāgatas*.

### *8. All-pervasiveness*

[49] All-pervasive means that buddha nature embraces everything with nothing left out. For example, space is all-pervasive: It is everywhere and contains everything. Of the two natures of the mind (emptiness and clarity) emptiness is compared to space. The clarity is given the name "immaculate space." Immaculate space is the name for Buddhahood and is all-pervasive in all beings.

[50] In logic there are general and particular characteristics of things. A general characteristic would be something like impermanence which applies to all phenomena. A particular characteristic would be like fire is hot and burning which doesn't apply to other phenomena. Buddha nature is a general characteristic of all beings irrespective of what qualities they possess. This is compared to space which pervades all forms and objects from very precious jewels to the most inferior objects such as rubbish—all of which have different particular characteristics.

### *9. Unalterability*

[51] One's faults are incidental to buddha nature and one's good qualities are an inherent part of buddha nature. The nature of buddha essence is that it never changes and has just temporary faults covering it up. The qualities are inherently present in buddh nature and manifest in enlightenment, rather than these qualities just begin to develop at the time of Buddhahood. So buddha nature is changeless and it is the same before and after Buddhahood.

[52] Unalterability in the phase of ordinary beings is unalterable for four reasons. First, it is like space which is void and pervades everything and there isn't one object in the universe that isn't permeated by space. Because the nature of space is extremely subtle, its nature is not altered by the objects whether it surrounds pure or polluted objects. From the beginning, buddha nature has been present in all beings but it was covered by the impurities of anger, jealousy, stupidity, etc. which don't affect the nature of this buddha nature. So buddha essence is unaffected by the impurities just as space is unaffected by the objects it contains.

[53] Second, if the nature is unalterable, consider all the universes which are made up of the elements. When the universe first begins, it has to manifest in space and when it disintegrates, it disintegrates in space. All this occurs in space, but space itself doesn't change or decompose. In the same way, buddha nature contains the five aggregates, elements, entrances, etc. and appearances which we experience. Everything arises and disintegrates in the uncreated space of buddha nature.

[54] Third, one may think the process of arising and disintegration may change the space so that it will be destroyed. But space has never been destroyed by fires. Since the beginning of time countless fires have never destroyed space. In the same way, buddha essence has never been burned out by the fires of death, sickness, and old age. On the relative level, there is the appearance of birth, sickness, and old age, but these do not affect buddha nature just as fire doesn't affect space.

[55] Fourth, buddha nature is unalterable. At the formation of the universe, the earth element rested on water and this ocean rested on a great circle of air and the air rests on space. So all the elements rest on space while space rested on nothing. All the five aggregates, the elements of thought, and the sense faculties rest on karma. They arise because there is karma—that is good and bad actions—and karma rests on the defilements of attachment, aggression, and ignorance. These defilements rest on a false view of the true nature of things. This false view of reality rests on the purity or true nature of the mind. But this true nature of the mind (buddha nature) like space doesn't rest on anything. So in this example the earth is similar to the five aggregates, the water is similar to karma and the defilements, air to an improper mode of thinking, and space to buddha nature.

[58] Earth is similar to the five aggregates, 12 entrances, and 18 elements. The five aggregates are form, feeling, cognition, mental formations, and consciousness. The earth is very coarse or dense and is the element that is the basis for life. In the same way the aggregates, elements, and entrances are the basis of our experiences of pleasure and pain. Water spreads everywhere on the earth and makes it

possible for plants to grow from the earth. In the same way, the positive and negative actions of our life determine the quality of our experiences and are motivated by defilements and a belief in a self. Water also is unstable because it moves and goes everywhere and in the same way the defilements also have this unstable way.

[59] Improper thinking is rooted in the basic ignorance of not realizing the essential nature of things. Because of this, delusion arises and is similar to air because air is very light and subtle, but animated by the slightest movement. Similarly, ignorance is very subtle and creates a very slight movement which stirs up karma and defilements.

[60] Improper thinking is not realizing the true nature of mind while proper thinking is to see phenomena correctly. In the example of seeing a rope in a dark place as a snake, the perception of a rope and snake have the same visual sensation. However, because of improper thinking, the rope is seen differently. So one can say this improper thinking rests on the nature of the mind and from it arises karma and the defilements. The actual nature of phenomena is peace and voidness and the absence of conceptual fabrication. Because one perceives true phenomena incorrectly, one incorrectly believes phenomena to be real. The first distortion occurs in perception of "self" and "others" and from this arises the feeling of attachment to "self" and a dislike of what is connected to others. From this distortion arises all the physical, mental, and verbal negative reactions. So the basis of this improper mode of thinking arises from karma.

[61] Karma and defilements manifest in all our experiences. Because of karma and defilements we are born in saṃsāra and experience the various sensations

based on the qualities of our karma. This is compared to the earth rising from the water element. The water contains many of particles of earth which arise to make solid earth. The solid substance will appear, but after a while it will disintegrate into the water element which gave birth to it. In the same way, the water of our karma and defilements arise from the aggregates, elements, and entrances of our experiences. Out of the water of our karma comes birth, old age, sickness, and death and we then sink into our karma to begin again.

[62] The true nature of the mind is compared to space because space is never created or destroyed. Likewise, the actual nature of the mind is changeless, clear, and not polluted by impurities. Space is not created by water or destroyed by fire and similarly buddha nature is not created by the water of karma and defilements or destroyed by the fire of old age, sickness, and death. The fires of death and old age are compared to the fires at of the end of time (hell fire) and ordinary fire respectively.

[66] Birth is acquiring a new set of aggregates in a particular life. Sickness and old age are alterations of the aggregates and death occurs when the aggregates terminate. The bodhisattvas are beyond old age, sickness, and death because they have realized the true nature of reality. Even though they are free from these four states, they do not try to liberate just themselves because this realization leads to a desire to free others. In more detail:

[67] Even though bodhisattvas give the appearance of birth, old age, sickness, and death, they do not experience suffering themselves. The realized ones, who have reached the bodhisattva levels have eliminated the root of birth, old age, sickness, and death because they have eliminated

karma. They have eliminated suffering and the experience of suffering because suffering is the fruition of the defilements. The bodhisattvas have the direct realization of voidness and clarity, therefore have transcended birth, old age, sickness, and death. Even though they are beyond this, they can see that other beings haven't realized this and this arouses compassion so they continue to manifest these four states.

[69] Taking each bodhisattva level, the text begins with the "sons of the victorious ones" who are all the followers of the Buddha. In this context the text refers to those who have reached the first bodhisattva level, that is those who have gained direct realization of the true nature of phenomena and realized buddha essence without distortion so they have the "eyes of jñāna." Others who don't have this realization are like the blind and the bodhisattvas remain to help these blind individuals. These bodhisattvas don't have to return and help others, but do so out of compassion.

[70] Those who have reached the level of the "realized ones" are in the next stage. The Tibetan word for "realized" is *pag pa* which literally means "higher." These are beings who have reached a higher state and the term refers to the first level of the bodhisattva. One reaches this domain when one reaches the path of insight which is the moment when phenomena are seen directly. An ordinary being may be on the path of accumulation or the path of junction. On these levels a person does not have this direct insight and therefore is called an "immature" being which in Tibetan means "infant." Ordinary beings are compared to infants because they cannot eat or take care of themselves. The difference between ordinary beings and

deeply realized beings rests completely on the absence of insight into the nature of reality. The realized bodhisattvas can manifest all the suffering in the domain of ordinary beings because they possess skillful means. This shows their realization is changeless and their suffering is an appearance to help others.

[71] Even though bodhisattvas in the second to seventh levels have transcended the defilements and karma, they do not depart from the world. When they work in the world, they do not become polluted by the defilements because they understand the true nature of phenomena. For example, a lotus grows in dirty water, but it is not dirty. In the same way, bodhisattvas are immersed in our world but they are not polluted by karma, defilements, or the suffering of our world.

[73] The main difference between bodhisattvas of the seventh and eighth level is that seventh level bodhisattvas have a slightly different experience between meditation and post-meditation. If you have dry wood, when lighted it catches fire automatically without effort. In the same way, bodhisattvas have great compassion so they automatically help other beings. Bodhisattvas on the eighth and ninth levels are constantly immersed in a state of balance, meditation on peace, so when they are helping others their minds are always in a perfect state of meditation. So there is no difference between their meditation and post-meditation.

[77] Bodhisattvas on the ninth level are very similar to bodhisattvas of the eighth level. Bodhisattvas on the tenth level have all the qualities of bodhisattvas on the eighth and ninth levels, but they are developed even further. As a result of their actions in previous lives, they have gathered

a great amount of virtue and spiritual energy and knowledge and can help beings without any effort or having to conceptualize "I must help" because they don't believe in the substantiality of objects. When they act, it is completely spontaneous like wood being placed on a fire. Even though this action is automatic, it is extremely precise so that by sitting, coming, and going they can teach the dharma. They chose a particular style that helps beings directly, know exactly when to act, and know how to act. Some beings, for example, need miracles and clairvoyance; others need only to observe very pure conduct; still others need only to hear the dharma. Buddha activity will come when it is needed, not a few days early or a few days later.

The activity of bodhisattvas on the tenth level goes everywhere and embraces everyone and is compared to space. There are uncountable beings everywhere and the extent of their negative karma is inconceivable. The activity of the bodhisattvas goes on continuously and manifests spontaneously. These bodhisattvas act without hindrances and interference of thoughts. They are in meditation all the time. The activities of these bodhisattvas are practically the same as the Buddhas. The difference, however, between a tenth level bodhisattvas and the Buddhas is the same as the difference between the earth and an atom or the difference between the ocean and water found in a hoof-print. There is a vast difference in the degree that they manifest.

[79] One may incorrectly think that when a bodhisattva has achieved the last stage of perfect Buddhahood, the buddha nature improves. But it doesn't change for four reasons. In the pure phase, buddha nature is the dharmakāya and all the qualities are present so it can't

change and therefore is permanent. It is eternal because Buddhahood is the constant refuge of beings and buddha activity won't end. The dharmakāya or stainless dharmadhātu is nondual because within it is the sameness of saṃsāra and nirvāṇa and all these qualities are pacified because there are no conceptual differences. The fourth quality is indestructibility because it is not created by defilements or karma. It is present from the beginning, has not been created, and therefore is indestructible. In more detail:

[80] Buddha nature is unalterable because it has no birth because it has no beginning, it has no death because it has no end, it is free from sickness because it doesn't change from good to bad, and it is free from old age because it is indestructible.

When Buddhahood is achieved, there is no change in the physical body; there is also no change in the subtle body. In Buddhahood there is no body. The word *kāya* literally means "body." In the nirmāṇakāya it looks as if the individual is taking birth and has a real body, but in the true sense it has an appearance of physical form. The dharmakāya is beyond the four extremes and eight fabrications so it has nothing to do with a body in the ordinary sense.

[81] Buddhahood is free from birth because it is permanent, it has no death because it is eternal. There is no death in the ordinary sense, but there is also the absence of even very subtle changes. This is why the Buddha can protect all beings and help all beings until the end of saṃsāra.

[82] Buddhahood is not harmed by sickness because it has peace which overcomes the duality of saṃsāra and

nirvāṇa. Since this dualistic division has ended, there is no suffering or sickness even from the fine karmic imprints that lead to a very subtle suffering. Buddhahood has no old age or degradation of the stream of existence. The Buddhas have no old age or degradation even in a subtle way from the untainted factors because Buddhahood is immutable.

[83] In summary, uncreated space refers to the emptiness aspect, while buddha nature refers to the clarity aspect. The name "buddha nature" shows it can bring forth all the qualities of the Buddha. So uncreated space has the attributes of permanence, eternity, peace, and immutability. Each refers to a different quality: the absence of birth to permanence; the absence of death to eternity; the absence of sickness to nonduality; and the absence of old age to immutability. So these qualities are unalterable.

[84] In the normal world good qualities wear out, but the qualities of Buddhahood are permanent because the body, speech, and mind of the Buddha are inexhaustible and changeless and therefore permanent. Vast numbers of beings on this earth are beset with negative karma causing an almost inexhaustible amount of impurities. For buddha activity to help purify these beings for as long as saṃsāra lasts requires that these qualities be eternal. It also has the nature of a refuge because it is there to help beings. The third quality is nonduality. Because in Buddhahood everything isn't divided into good and bad, it is beyond this and therefore in a state of peace. The last is the quality of indestructibility because it never vanishes because the qualities of Buddhahood are not fabricated.

At the impure level of ordinary beings the aggregates and the four elements change while buddha nature is changeless as described in the example of space. In the mixed phase buddha essence remained changeless even though bodhisattvas work to help all beings. In the phase of total purity the buddha essence is changeless even though the Buddhas help all beings. So buddha essence is changeless.

### *10. Inseparability of the Qualities*

Buddha nature is given four different names: the dharmakāya, tathāgata, highest truth, and supreme nirvāṇa. It is called the "dharmakāya" because it is the true nature of all things. It is called the "tathāgata" because it is the ultimate fruition of seeing what is there. It is called the truth of the realized ones or the "highest truth" because the realized ones see phenomena as-it-is. It is called the "ultimately true nirvāṇa" because it is beyond the suffering of saṃsāra.

The inseparability of the four qualities is similar to the sun and the sunshine because one cannot have one without the other. The dharmakāya, the tathāgata, the highest truth, and the supreme nirvāṇa are inseparable at the stage of ordinary beings, bodhisattvas, and Buddhas. When Buddhahood is achieved, there is no other nirvāṇa beyond that and no other truths. In more detail:

[85] Untainted space is divided into the four aspects of the dharmakāya, the tathāgata, the highest truth, and ultimate nirvāṇa. The dharmakāya is the sum of all the qualities of the Buddha (the ten powers, four fearlessnesses, etc.) and these are inseparable. The term "tathāgata" is used to show that from the beginning of time the buddha causal ground has been within all beings. The term "highest truth" shows that the true nature is always present

and contains no falsehoods. The term "nirvāṇa" means beyond suffering because this nature is free from all impurities so there is no pain or suffering.

[87] In the fruition of Buddhahood all the aspects of knowledge are the Buddha. All the aspects of knowledge means achieving knowledge of how-it-is and the knowledge of variety and also totally removing of all impurities and karmic imprints. The ı timate achievement is represented with Buddhahood being complete knowledge and nirvāṇa being complete purity. Buddhahood and nirvāṇa are not separate, however, in the ultimate sense.

[88] Liberation is the direct realization of phenomena by seeing it as-they-are. Liberation has the characteristics of being inseparable, numberless, unthinkable, and stainless. All these qualities are complete in the dharmakāya.

The first example illustrates that when some of the parts are missing, the whole cannot exist. The second example shows the inseparability of different parts of a whole.

[89] Imagine some artists, each skilled in painting just one part of the body so that one artist can draw, for example, the eyes; another can draw just the arms, another just the hair, etc. Now a king gathers these artists together and gives them a canvas and asks them to do his portrait. In the middle of the painting, one of the artists leaves the country so that the portrait can't be completed.

[92] Similarly, Buddhahood is similar to the completed picture with each artist representing the different qualities necessary to achieve Buddhahood. If all the qualities of the six pāramitās are present, then all the conditions for reaching Buddhahood are there and voidness can be apprehended directly. The voidness with all the aspects is

like the fully completed portrait of the king. The voidness is not emptiness, but the great fullness of these qualities with the quality of clarity in which all these aspects of knowledge can flourish. For this voidness to be realized all the qualities of the pāramitās have to be present just as all the artists have to be present to complete the portrait.

[93] The inseparability of the qualities of prajñā, jñāna, and freedom is illustrated by the sun. The Tibetan word for "prajñā" is *sherab* and this literally means "better knowledge" so prajñā means the understanding without distortion both of the nominal and phenomenal aspect of things. Jñāna (Tib. *yeshe*) is very clear cognition and is used for the cognition of the essential or nominal aspect of things. One doesn't use jñāna for gaining knowledge about a river or a mountain, but reserves this for knowledge about the true nature of things. These two qualities are present as seeds in ordinary beings and are fully manifest at Buddhahood. When the impurities at the stage of ordinary beings are removed, the third quality of perfect freedom emerges. Prajñā, jñāna, and freedom from impurities are compared to sunlight, sun rays, and the orb of the sun and are luminous, radiant, and pure respectively.

[94] Nirvāṇa is not possible without the jñāna of the Buddha. The example states that without sunlight and the sun's rays the sun cannot be seen. So the qualities of the Buddha are inseparable.

## Table 2
## A Summary of the Ten Qualities of Buddha Nature

*1. The nature of buddha nature is inherently pure like:*

| | |
|---|---|
| a. a jewel | (has power) |
| b. the sky | (is changeless) |
| c. water | (compassion) |

*2. The four causes that allow buddha nature to manifest:*

| | |
|---|---|
| a. aspiration | (to overcome dislike of dharma) |
| b. prajñā | (to overcome belief in self) |
| c. samādhi | (to overcome fear of samsāra) |
| d. compassion | (to overcome selfishness) |

*3. Once there is fruition of buddha nature which is beyond saṃsāra and nirvāṇa, one has the qualities of:*

| | |
|---|---|
| a. true purity | (counteract impurities due to karma) |
| b. true identity | (counteract suffering in life) |
| c. true happiness | (counter impermanence of skandhas) |
| d. true permanence | (counteracts belief in self) |

*4. The function or influence of buddha nature is:*

a. One develops a weariness of saṃsāra

b. One can then see the benefits of nirvāṇa

*5. The endowments of buddha nature are:*

Example of the ocean on the path

| | |
|---|---|
| a. dharmakāya | (vastness of ocean) |
| b. two-fold jñāna | (jewels in the ocean) |
| c. compassion | (wetness of ocean) |

Example of the butter lamp at fruition

| | |
|---|---|
| a. clear cognition | (light of the lamp) |
| b. stainless jñāna | (heat of the lamp) |
| c. clarity | (color of the lamp) |

*6. The approach of beings to buddha nature is:*

a. ordinary beings use the incorrect approach

b. bodhisattvas go in the right direction
c. Buddhas are unerring and non-conceptually right

7. *The phases of buddha nature are:*
a. impure (in ordinary beings)
b. mixed (in the bodhisattvas)
c. pure (in the tathāgatas)

8. *The all-pervasiveness of buddha nature is:*
In example of space:
a. pervades all but unaffected by it
b. all arises and disintegrates in it with no effect
c. it is never consumed by fires of birth, old age, etc.

9. *Buddha nature is unalterable because it has:*
In the example of ordinary beings:
a. earth (the aggregates, elements, and senses)
b. water (karma and the defilements)
c. air (incorrect understanding)
d. space (clarity)
In the example of the bodhisattvas:
a. beyond birth (quality of permanence)
b. beyond ageing (quality of immutability)
c. beyond sickness (quality of nonduality)
d. beyond death (quality of being eternal)
In the example of the Buddhas:
a. permanent (the Buddhas are changeless)
b. eternal (there is inexhaustible negative karma)
c. nondual (inseparability of samsāra and nirvāṇa)
d. indestructible (Buddhahood is not fabricated)

10. *The qualities are inseparable because:*
a. dharmakāya (true nature of all things)
b. tathāgata (ultimate fruition)
c. highest truth (knowledge of how-it-is)
d. supreme nirvāṇa (beyond suffering)

# CHAPTER 7

# BUDDHA NATURE II:
## *The Nine Examples*

One may still have doubts about how buddha nature is changeless, but does not manifest because of impurities. To illustrate this nine examples of buddha essence and the impurities are given.

### *Examples of Buddha Nature*

When the Buddha gave teachings, he didn't simply declare the truth, but he gave reasons for what he was saying. The reasons for his teachings were sometimes very apparent and at other times very obscure. The obvious teachings were the ones grasped by the senses. There are, however, teachings which cannot be grasped with sensory faculties because they were about things very far away, or very remote in time, or about karma. A particular karma will prevent one from living certain types of lives. Since one cannot understand these more hidden meanings directly, one has to understand them through inference. For instance, if we say there's a fire behind that hill because we can see smoke, people believe it even though they can't see the actual fire because smoke is a valid sign of a fire. For a sign to be significant it must have universal applicability i.e., whenever there is a fire, there must be smoke. The sign must also be valid, if we say there's a fire because I see a tree, it is an invalid sign. So a sign for showing the presence of something that is hidden must have universal applicability and be a valid sign. The presence of buddha essence is illustrated with signs using nine examples. Then this reasoning is applied to buddha nature itself.

[96] The nine examples of beautiful things covered up by impurities are listed along with the nine impurities followed by a list of the pure things covered up. These will be elaborated below. The method for presenting each example is the same: first a verse gives the example, then a verse gives its meaning, and finally a verse presents the parallel between the example and buddha nature.

[99] Imagine an ugly, withered lotus covering a beautiful buddha statue. Someone with clairvoyance could see the statue and think that this was not a good place for such a beautiful statue and would break open the lotus shell and remove the statue. Similarly, buddha nature is in the mind of all beings, even those in the worst hell, but it is obscured by the defilements of the three poisons. The Buddhas with divine vision and great compassion see this buddha essence and help beings out of the shell of defilements. Individuals with buddha nature need to reach Buddhahood so they do not continue to suffer in saṃsāra; therefore they need the Buddhas with their vision and their teachings to receive the tools to make this buddha nature manifest.

[102] Imagine some tasty honey which is surrounded by swarming bees. If an experienced person knows how to separate the honey from the bees, then people can enjoy the honey. This means the Buddhas with the omniscient eyes of twofold knowledge can see the buddha nature in all beings which is like the honey. The bees circling the honey

can be removed because they aren't part of the honey. In the same way, the impurities of beings aren't part of their buddha nature and therefore can be removed allowing buddha nature to manifest. In this example, the man who knows about honey is like the Buddhas who are skilled in removing obscurations, which are the bees.

[105] Imagine a grain of rice enclosed in its husk. Kernels of rice, buckwheat, and barley cannot be used as food when they are unhusked. Similarly, as long as buddha nature called "the lord of all qualities" is not liberated from the shell of impurities, it cannot give the taste of the joy of dharma to beings.

[108] Imagine an individual going on a journey and on his way he loses some pure gold which falls into some rubbish. It remains unchanged for hundreds of years being quite useless. Then a god with clairvoyance sees the large lump of gold in the rubbish and tells someone where to find it so it can be put to proper use.

[110] Similarly, the Buddhas can see the pure buddha nature of beings which has fallen into the filth of defilements and has been lying there for thousands of years. Even though it is there, it has not been polluted by the defilements. If there were no rubbish there is the first place, there would be no need to have the clairvoyant person come along. Also if there had been no gold for the clairvoyant person to point out, it would have been pointless as well. Similarly, if buddha nature were not obscured by defilements, there would be no need for the Buddhas to enter this world and teach about buddha nature. Also if beings didn't have buddha nature from the very beginning, there would be no need for the Buddhas to give teachings because it would be impossible for individuals to

attain Buddhahood. This is why the Buddhas give teachings and point out our obscurations. They do this by producing the rain of dharma which has the ability to gradually wash away the impurities which we have accumulated.

Gold is very useful, but if it is covered by rubbish it is useless. This is why this clairvoyant person tells someone where it is and tells him to remove the rubbish and use the gold. In the same way, the Buddhas tell us about the rubbish of our instability. They see beings who have the wish-fulfilling gem in their hands, wasting it. Beings are suffering, but they have the tool to eliminate the suffering and this is why the Buddhas teach the dharma. Beings remain stuck in problems and difficulties and don't have the power to realize their own goal. They might think there is nothing they can do, but they have the knowledge of how-it-is and variety, so they have everything necessary to remove the defilements. The Buddha told them that if they practice, they can reach enlightenment.

[112] Imagine a man so poor that he doesn't have any food or clothes, living in a house built over a great treasure. If the man doesn't know about the treasure, he will continue to suffer in poverty because the treasure cannot say, "Look, I am here." Similarly, all beings have the great treasure of buddha nature in their minds and this treasure has always been there. They do not see the buddha essence in their mind so they endure all the sufferings of saṃsāra. The treasure can't tell the man "I am here" even though it is very close by. Similarly, all beings have the precious treasure of the dharmakāya locked in their mind, but continue to suffer. Therefore the great sages, the Buddhas, come into our world to help beings find this treasure.

[115] A very tiny seed in a fruit has the power to be an enormous tree. One cannot see the tree in the seed, but if one adds all the right conditions for growth such as water, sunlight, soil, etc. to the seed, a mighty tree will develop. Similarly, buddha essence exists in all beings but is encased in the peel of ignorance which generates our emotional and cognitive obscurations. If one practises virtue, it will generate the favorable conditions for this seed of buddha nature to grow. Through the accumulation of knowledge and virtue, the seed will develop into the "king of victors" or Buddhahood. The parallel is that just as a tree with the proper conditions grows from a seed enclosed by the skin of a fruit into a tree, buddha essence is enclosed in the skin of defilements and with proper conditions will manifest into Buddhahood.

[118] Imagine a very valuable buddha statue wrapped in tattered rags and abandoned by the side of the road. A passerby would not notice it, but if a god came along, he could see the statue. Similarly, the Buddhas with their jñāna can see that buddha nature of beings is wrapped in the tattered rags of the defilements. They see this in persons and even in animals. As a god can see a statue with divine vision, the Buddhas can see buddha nature lying on the road of saṃsāra inside the rags of defilements. They tell beings to remove the tattered rags so the buddha nature can manifest in its complete purity.

[121] Imagine a destitute ugly woman with no place to stay who ends up in a pauper's hostel. Also imagine that she is pregnant and holds in her womb the future king. She continues to suffer because she doesn't know anything about it. Similarly, beings hold the precious buddha essence but do not know anything about it or get any

benefit from it. As the woman in the hostel has a king in her womb so beings are born in the six realms of saṃsāra; some as humans, some as animals, some as hungry ghosts, etc. All have to suffer—animals suffer from enslavement, spirits have to suffer from thirst and hunger, humans have to suffer from birth, sickness, old age, and death. All are like the poor woman living in misery.

[123] The poor woman with a great ruler in her womb is dressed in dirty clothes. Because she doesn't know that she bears a king, she remains in poverty and is very unhappy. In the same way, beings have a protector inside their mind, but are unaware of this so they have no peace of mind and are overpowered by defilements; thus they remain in saṃsāra and undergo all kinds of suffering.

[124] Imagine a very pure statue covered with a crust of clay. Someone who knew about this could remove the clay and reveal the gold statue. In the same way, the clear light nature of the mind is inside us, but covered with impurities. These impurities are not permanent and can be removed like the clay crust covering the beautiful statue. Someone knowing that the clay is covering the statue can remove the clay gradually to reveal the gold statue. In the same way, the omniscient bodhisattvas know with their jñāna that buddha essence is inside beings and through teaching the dharma they can gradually remove all the impurities covering the pure mind.

[127] These nine examples show that all beings have buddha essence, but it doesn't manifest because it is covered by impurities. The Buddhas can see the buddha essence and therefore they teach the dharma on how to remove the impurities. Because of buddha nature, one can reach Buddhahood with purification.

In summary, there were nine examples of the impurities. If one had a white shell, for example, one can't separate the whiteness from the roundness of the shell. But buddha nature is completely separate from the impurities so these impurities can be separated when buddha nature manifests.

[130] Each of the nine examples corresponds to one of the defilements and a level of the path. To summarize:

1. In the example of the lotus, the shell corresponds to attachment found in ordinary beings.
2. In the example of the bee swarm, the bees correspond to aggression found in ordinary beings.
3. In the example of withered rice, the husk corresponds to ignorance found in ordinary beings.
4. In the example of gold in rubbish, the filth corresponds to attachment, aggression, and ignorance in a very active state found in ordinary beings.
5. In the example of buried treasure, the soil corresponds to the latent karmic traces of attachment, aggression, and ignorance left behind in arhats.
6. In the example of fruit, the skin corresponds to fabricated obscurations worked on by those on the path of insight by bodhisattvas on the mahāyāna path.
7. In the example of the statue in rags, the rags correspond to the innate obscurations worked on by those on the path of cultivation by bodhisattvas on the mahāyāna path.
8. In the example of the pregnant woman, her womb represents the impurities of the bodhisattva in the first to seventh bodhisattva levels.
9. In the example of the statue in clay, the clay represents the impurities of the bodhisattva in the eighth to tenth bodhisattva levels. In more detail:

[134] A lotus is a beautiful flower which grows out of mud. When one sees a lotus blooming, it is very beautiful and one is happy seeing it. Later when it withers, one's pleasure disappears. In a similar way, desire comes out of the mind of saṃsāra and when something desirable or attractive first presents itself, it might bring pleasure, but with time it loses its appeal and becomes suffering.

[135] Bees are very attached to their honey; when the honey is touched they become very angry or irritated and give pain to others by stinging them. So when the bees are hurt, they hurt others. In the same way, when one is angry, one is very irritable and one hurts others with harsh words or actions.

[136] Grains such as rice are covered with a husk which obscures the grain inside. In the same way, ignorance keeps one from seeing the true nature of phenomena. It is a thick covering like a shell or husk which prevents one from seeing what is there.

[137] Filth or rubbish covering gold is very unpleasant and disagreeable. In the same way when attachment, aggression, and ignorance are very strong, they are very repulsive and also increase one's attachment to pleasures.

[138] The soil covers the treasure so that one does not know a treasure is there. In the same way, very fine mental imprints caused by ignorance are present in the mind. This is the innate ignorance present since the beginning of time saṃsāra which covers up the true nature of the mind so one cannot recognize its true nature.

[139] When one is on the path to enlightenment as an ordinary being, one is on the path of accumulation and the path of junction. One practices because one has a goal of practice, but little direct realization. After a while one gets

a direct insight into the nature of phenomena and becomes a bodhisattva who sees "the rope as a rope" and all misconceptions are relinquished. This is the path of cultivation of insight which is compared to a shoot growing from the skin of a fruit. When one has reached this path of insight, jñāna starts to manifest.

[140] On the path of insight, the obscurations are eliminated but we don't automatically reach Buddhahood. We have been in saṃsāra for such a long time that we have acquired very strong mental habits. The gross misconceptions have been removed, but the innate ignorance from the very beginning still remains as a trace. After we have the insight, we need to cultivate this insight until it becomes very firm. This path of cultivation is called the path of the realized ones. It is the time when the core of the belief of self (called the "multitude of fears" because it causes great fear) is removed. This is compared to tattered rags which are so rotten they are quite easy to remove. In the same way, these mental impurities are quite soft, subtle, and easy to remove.

[141] The eighth example corresponds to the impurities in the first seven bodhisattva levels. These are compared to a baby in the womb. The baby must wait there nine months and with each day it knows it is closer to being born. Similarly, a bodhisattva at each stage is growing more complete as impurities are removed with jñāna maturing more and more.

[142] The ninth example relates to the very fine impurities of the last three bodhisattva levels which have to be eliminated. These are compared to traces of clay covering a statue. These great beings, the bodhisattvas on the tenth level, remove these slight impurities through

vajra-like samādhi. This is compared to a vajra because it is very powerful and solid; it can destroy everything else and not be destroyed itself.

[144] There is a purity aspect of each of the nine examples. Buddha nature is the union of three natures: dharmakāya, the suchness, and causal ground. The dharmakāya refers to the clarity aspect, the suchness to voidness, and the causal ground to the aspect of full manifestation. If one has a shell that is white and round, one can say that from the color aspect it is white, from the shape aspect it is round; however, the whiteness and roundness are inseparable. In the same way the clarity, voidness, and the causal ground which are the ability to manifest as Buddhahood are also inseparable. Of the nine examples there are three examples for the dharmakāya, one example for the suchness, and five for the causal ground.

[145] The first three examples relate to the dharmakāya. The dharmakāya can be divided into the actual dharmakāya and the relative dharmakāya which is also called dharmakāya, but is not really the dharmakāya. The true dharmakāya is the stainless dharmadhātu, the actual buddha nature, which is by nature luminosity and in the domain of self-cognisant jñāna. Relative dharmakāya is called the "teaching dharmakāya" which are the scriptures that teach the meaning of the dharmakāya. These scriptures have a deep aspect related to the dharmakāya and a vast aspect related to the various mentalities of beings.

[146] The first example is of the true dharmakāya which cannot be fathomed so it is represented by the Buddha in a withering lotus.[5]

[5] Thrangu Rinpoche believes that in this case it is the Buddha himself, not a statue of the Buddha.

[147] The second example of honey represents the teaching dharmakāya because the taste of honey is very subtle, as are the teachings of the dharmakāya. Honey is always very sweet and all kinds of honey have this same sweet taste. In comparison, all the various phenomena of the dharmakāya have one taste or a similar nature. The third example of grain in husks, the millions of grains represent the great variety of teachings. The deep aspect of the teaching is represented by the honey, the vast aspect is represented by the grains in the husk.

[148] The fourth example of gold illustrates the changeless character of the suchness. Suchness is not completely pure and not changed by suffering or defilements. It is perfectly pure and therefore is compared to gold which has the same qualities.

[149] The last five examples refer to causal ground. The causal ground is compared to a treasure because a treasure can lie beneath the ground for hundreds of years and remain unchanged. The causal ground is compared to a fruit because when a fruit is still a fruit one cannot see the tree, but the fruit contains the potential of a tree. The example of a treasure describes the innate aspect of the causal ground and the example of the fruit describes how the proper practice of virtue can manifest into Buddhahood. These two aspects of the causal ground develop into the three kāyas of the Buddha. The dharmakāya is the outcome of the innate aspect and the form kāyas are the outcome of the practice of virtue.

[151] The essence kāya, svābhāvikakāya or dharmakāya, is compared to an example of a buddha statue made of precious substances. The innate aspect of causal ground is compared to a treasure of jewels because it is there

naturally. The sambhogakāya is compared to a great king or cakravatin because the sambhogakāya is endowed with the great power of dharma. The nirmāṇakāya is illustrated by a golden statue because it is a representation of the Buddha.

[153] As an ordinary person one cannot understand Buddha essence directly and therefore needs the help of faith to understand it. The buddha nature has been there from the very beginning and was never created by anyone. It is the spontaneously present jñāna. An ordinary person cannot see this directly because his buddha nature is covered by impurities. He or she may be able to gain some indirect understanding of it by inference, but even this is hard to understand because it is in the domain of the inconceivable. For example, the sun sheds its brilliant rays all the time; as far as the sun is concerned, it never is obscured by anything. But a blind person will never see this sunshine. In the same way, the spontaneously present jñāna has been there from the very beginning but it is hidden from ordinary beings who do not have the clear eyes of prajñā to see through the thick darkness of ignorance. They must rely on faith in order to understand this buddha nature.

Buddha essence has two kinds of purity: it is naturally pure, and is pure from incidental impurities. It has always had these qualities, but when one doesn't see this fully one makes mistakes, goes astray, and wanders in saṃsāra.

[155] Buddha nature is void and not void in a way. The buddha essence is devoid of any passing impurity because these are not an intrinsic part of it. On the other hand, the buddha essence is not devoid of the supreme qualities because the qualities are an inseparable part of the actual nature of the buddha essence.

### *Importance of Buddha Nature*

The fourth major division in this chapter on buddha nature explains why it is necessary to teach about the presence of the buddha nature and what benefits one can expect from understanding this teaching.

To review, the Buddha turned the wheel of dharma three times. The second turning demonstrated the voidness of all phenomena. In these teachings the Buddha said there is no form, sound, taste, smell, etc. with everything being devoid of any actual nature. Everything is void beyond the four extremes of existence and nonexistence and beyond the eight mental fabrications. Everything is the dharmadhātu devoid of any actual nature of its own. In the third turning, Buddha stated all beings had buddha nature and he described the nature of the buddha nature in detail. Ordinary beings might think that there is a contradiction between teachings of the second turning in which the Buddha said there wasn't anything and in the third turning in which he said there was.

[156] In the text it states that the Buddha taught phenomena are devoid of actual nature; they are like a cloud, a dream, or an illusion. This was explained in many sūtras in the long, middle, and short form of the *Prajñāpāramitā* sūtra. The Buddha in this teaching stated that anything knowable is devoid of any actual nature; that is, it is always void and always has been void. In the third turning the Buddha said that all beings have Buddha essence which appears to contradict the second turning teachings.

[157] The answer to this contraction is that if we do not understand the presence of Buddha nature in all beings, we

will make five mistakes in reasoning. The first mistake is faintheartedness; we will become discouraged about the possibility of attaining Buddhahood. We will think the Buddhas of the past have managed to attain Buddhahood, but they were individuals quite different from ourself, so Buddhahood is totally out of reach. If we think this way, we may not even begin to work for liberation. The second mistake is we don't know that other beings have buddha nature and we might feel contempt for persons who have a lesser understanding than our own and believe they have no chance of achieving Buddhahood. The third mistake is to have misconceptions of the true nature of things and believe appearances are real. Fourth, if we don't understand that all beings have buddha nature and therefore have the possibility of reaching Buddhahood, we might think that beings are simply empty and void and we might therefore ridicule their true nature. If we do not understand all beings are alike because they all possess buddha nature, we may make the fifth mistake of thinking more highly of ourself than others. We therefore spend more time looking for happiness for ourself and less in helping others. To prevent these five mistakes the Buddha gave three teachings.

[158] The ultimate nature of everything is devoid of anything composite. In this true nature there is no such thing as form, sound, sight, etc. because it is beyond both existence and non-existence, the four extremes, and the eight conceptual fabrications. In the ultimate sense everything is voidness, but in the relative sense everything manifests because of the defilements, karma, and the fruition of karma.

[159] These three causes of manifestation are compared to clouds, a dream, and an illusion respectively. In the second turning, all relative manifestation are described as an illusion but in the ultimate sense all phenomena are void. The defilements of attachment, aggression, ignorance, and belief in a self are compared to clouds which cover buddha essence. These defilements give rise to our good and bad actions (karma) which are tainted by the presence of defilements. These actions are compared to the experiences we have in dreams. Although sounds, forms, feelings, and so on appear to us as real in a dream, they have no reality in themselves. This is the same for everything we experience. As a result of defilements and karma there is the maturation of the five aggregates. A great magician with different tricks can conjure up different illusions. These illusions are produced by the magician, but they do not have any actual independent reality. In the same way, all aggregates and manifestations of existence are conjured up by the defilements and karma and are like an illusion with no independent reality. The second turning made clear that on the ultimate level everything is void, but on the relative level everything manifests to us like clouds or dreams or illusions.

[160] The purpose of this teaching was to eliminate five misconceptions which arise from not knowing about buddha nature. The first mistake is discouragement or faintheartedness which is a form of self-contempt. It appears when one thinks one is unable to do something because one is not good enough to do it. We think, "I cannot get rid of the defilements; I cannot achieve Buddhahood and help beings and practice dharma" and lack the confidence to practice. In general, when someone

doesn't have enough confidence in worldly affairs, they cannot accomplish what they have to do. This is also true of the dharma; if we don't have enough courage, we aren't able to generate the state of mind conducive to enlightenment. A bodhisattva must have compassion and understanding. Without self-confidence, the bodhisattva won't be able to practice along these lines.

[162] If we are able to generate some bodhicitta, then others who don't have this motivation appear inferior. So to think, "I'm much better than others because they don't have strong motivation" and to develop strong pride and look down on others is the second mistake because everyone has buddha nature.

[163] The third mistake is to lack the right kind of understanding and to believe phenomenal appearances to be real. We cling to this misconception, because we do not understand that all phenomenal appearances are empty.

[164] The faults and defects in beings are only transient and fabrications. Actually, within individuals all the qualities are pure and present. If we don't understand this, we will speak ill of the true nature which is the fourth fault.

[165] The fifth mistake of not knowing that all beings possess buddha nature and to value oneself over all beings. The opposite is characteristic of bodhisattvas who love others as much as themselves. If we don't know about buddha nature, one cannot achieve this complete love.

[166] If we know about the presence of buddha nature, the five mistakes can be dispelled. On hearing the teaching of Buddha nature we will not be discouraged; on the contrary we will be happy to learn there is no need to continue in samsāra because we possess this essence of Buddhahood and has the power to achieve Buddhahood in

the future. We will be joyous because we discover we are on the path with all the Buddhas of the past, present, and future and is able to achieve enlightenment because we have the cause of it in ourself.

The second benefit of this teaching is that we will develop respect for all beings. Because all beings are potential Buddhas, we cannot despise them, but can only feel respect for them. The knowledge of buddha nature will also dispel the three remaining faults. Knowing all persons possess buddha nature allows us to stop believing the reality of phenomena. At first we believe everything is empty and believe in this reality. Knowledge of buddha nature gives rise to prajñā which is the understanding of the true nature of things. Understanding that buddha nature is possessed by all beings gives birth to jñāna. Finally, loving kindness will develop as a result of giving up egotism or valuing oneself over others.

[167] With the growth of these five good qualities, the five unwholesome qualities will be abandoned and we will understand that all beings are the same in that they all possess the buddha essence and have the power to achieve Buddhabood. When we know this, we will develop loving kindness towards beings making it possible to achieve Buddhahood quickly.

# CHAPTER 8

## *Enlightenment*

The explanation of the fifth vajra point is similar in structure to the outline of the chapter on buddha nature. There will be a summary of eight points concerning enlightenment and then each of these points will be presented in greater detail.

### *Characteristics of Enlightenment*

[168] One has to enter the path that leads to enlightenment and when this path reaches completion, one acnieves Buddhahood. The first point is the nature of enlightenment which is purity because no obscurations are left. The second point is that on the path one studies, reflects, and practices meditation and when these practices have sufficiently developed, one achieves Buddhahood. The third point is once one is completely free from obscurations, one is free from anything to be relinquished. The fourth point is called function and this is to create the best possible outcome for oneself and others. Reaching enlightenment is the best possible outcome because one will never have to return to samsāra and suffer again. This is of great value to others because it will help an incalculable number of other beings reach the same state. The fifth point describes the various qualities which are the basis for the twofold realization that leads to

enlightenment. The sixth point is the way in which enlightenment manifests through the qualities of depth, vastness, and greatness of nature which are related to the three kāyas. Depth relates to the dharmakāya which represents the true nature of all phenomena. Vastness relates to the sambhogakāya because it can act in a great variety of ways. Greatness of nature relates to the nirmāṇakāya because this is by nature very pure and works to help beings. The seventh point describes enlightenment in terms of how long this activity goes on. The last point refers to the actual nature of phenomena which relates to its inconceivability.

[169] Each of these aspects is defined through the various facets they represent. Purity represents the nature of enlightenment; achievement represents the result of the path; freedom from all impurities represents the fruition of the path. Value for oneself and others represents the function of enlightenment. The basis for the twofold value are all the qualities present at enlightenment. The depth, vastness, and greatness of nature refer to the dharmakāya, sambhogakāya and nirmāṇakāya respectively and the way in which these kāyas manifest. The duration of these kāyas represents permanence. The actual nature is defined as being inconceivable.

### *Nature and Cause of Enlightenment*

[170] The nature of enlightenment represents purity and the cause of enlightenment are the conditions necessary to achieve enlightenment. Buddha essence is by nature clear light (Tib. *ösel*) which means that by nature it is completely pure. Even for ordinary beings buddha nature

is pure in nature. When it manifests at enlightenment, it is free from incidental stains by the four particularities.

The first three particularities refer to the nature of enlightenment and the fourth to a causal condition for enlightenment. The first particularity is lucid clarity and is compared to the sun. The sun refers to the essence, and sky refers to the nature. This example of sun and space refers to the two facets of enlightenment. The sun refers to knowledge and sky refers to purity from all obscurations. This is parallel to the Tibetan word for the Buddha which is *sang gay*. *Sang* means "completely pure" referring to the purity aspect, while *gay* means "awakened" from the sleep of ignorance referring to the realization aspect.

The second particularity is purity which literally means "having relinquished all impurities." The emotional and cognitive obscurations are compared to clouds covering the sun. The third particularity is possession of buddha qualities. The Buddha has all the qualities of freedom and the qualities of maturity which are not temporary, but eternal and unchanging. When one reaches Buddhahood there is a causal condition of both the nonconceptual and analytical jñāna to make achievement possible. When Buddhahood is achieved, one has the knowledge of how-it-is (nonconceptual jñāna) and variety (analytical jñāna). At the level of a bodhisattva these two jñānas are already present and working but become fully developed in Buddhahood. The nonconceptual jñāna functions during meditation when one obtains direct insight into the true nature of phenomena. Analytical jñāna functions during post-meditation when one learns about the great variety of relative phenomena. By means of these two aspects of jñāna Buddhahood is achieved. In more detail:

[171] The first particularity concerns the nature of enlightenment. Previously, this point was compared to the sun and sky with the sun representing the clarity of jñāna and the sky representing the purity that comes from relinquishing all incidental impurities. Buddhahood is indivisible which means that it cannot be separated from the buddha nature. It is also perfectly pure, having the purity of nature and the purity of complete elimination of impurities. So this jñāna is like the sun and this freedom from impurities is like space.

[172] The second point is that the qualities are inseparable from each other. It is said that the clear light is uncreated and the buddha essence is by nature clarity so this clarity is inherent. This clarity pervades all beings without any differentiation and these good qualities are greater than the number of grains of sand in the river Ganges.

[173] Third, although impurities are actually nonexistent (void), they are present in ordinary beings like clouds covering the sun. Clouds appearing in the sky do not belong to the nature of the sky, but are only incidental to it. Similarly, the tarnish on a piece of gold is not part of the gold; but something that can be removed because it isn't an intrinsic part of its nature.

Because these impurities are not part of buddha nature, they can be removed. These impurities are defined as nonexistent, spreading everywhere, and being incidental. Similarly, clouds represent the two obscurations veiling buddha essence; when they are removed Buddhahood manifests in its full purity.

[174] The fourth point is that these obscurations can be removed by means of the two jñānas. The manifestation of

buddha nature is similar to when the clouds have been removed, the sun is visible again. The emotional obscurations are hiding the liberation aspect and the cognitive obscurations are hiding the omniscient aspect of Buddhahood. These two jñānas of how-it-is and variety manifest gradually until they are fully matured to enlightenment. Knowledge of how-it-is develops from non-conceptual meditation on the nature of all phenomena understanding their void nature.

Post-meditation allows the jñāna of variety to manifest showing what is relevant at the relative level (called the "vast" aspect of phenomena) and what belongs to the ultimate level (called the "deep" aspect of phenomena). This dispels the cognitive obscurations. So on the development of the path these two qualities become manifest so that the obscurations can be removed and Buddhahood can manifest.

### *3. Fruition of Enlightenment*

There are two logical ways fruition of enlightenment can occur. It can be created by something else or it can be the result of removing a covering. In the *Uttara Tantra* it says purification occurs by removing obscurations. If the qualities of the Buddha were acquired instead, they would be composite in nature and subject to change. However, they are originally present in the mind of all beings and therefore can't be acquired.

[175] Freedom from the kleśa of desire is compared to the simile of a lake covered by lotuses. Freedom from anger uses the simile of the moon freed from being eaten by Rahu (Rahu is a symbol for an eclipse). Freedom from ignorance uses the simile of the sun and clouds.

[176] The nine examples of the previous chapter are, first of all, given to illustrate that Buddhahood is like the body of the Buddha, honey can be used after being taken away from the bees, kernels of the grains can be eaten once the husk has been removed, etc. In more detail:

[177] The purity achieved by nonconceptual and post-meditation jñāna is the fruition of purification from emotional obscurations. This is described with three examples of a lake overgrown with lotuses, an eclipse, and clouds hiding the sun. When these are removed, one can see the pure waters of the lake, the full moon, and the sun respectively. In the same way, when the defilements are removed, one can see the buddha essence clearly without any emotional obscurations. Non-conceptual jñāna, which is the direct realization of the true nature of phenomena, makes it possible to remove these emotional obscurations. This jñāna has no concept of how things are; it just perceives phenomena just as they are.

[178] When the cognitive obscurations are removed, one can achieve the supremely endowed buddha kāyas. They are removed through the post-meditation jñāna which perceives all phenomena in all their variety without confusion. So during meditation, one sees the true nonexistent character of everything directly and during post-meditation one sees the great variety of illusions in which beings are immersed. This particular post-meditation jñāna will erase the cognitive obscurations so that all the buddha kāyas can manifest.

[179] The next point shows how the fruition of Buddhahood is free from the three poisons. In the example of the lake, persons are compared to lotuses and these "lotuses" are made pure from the silt of desire by the pure waters of meditation.

[180] The second example is of the moon obscured by an eclipse. Normally, the moon's light is very bright, cooling, and soothing. During an eclipse it becomes reddish, then black, and is no longer beautiful and bright. Similarly, there is a very strong change that takes place when somebody is under the influence of anger. A very peaceful and loving person turns into an unkind person and develops the wish to hurt others when under the influence of anger. So this anger eclipses his natural good qualities. When someone is liberated from anger, it is like the full moon coming out of an eclipse.

[181] The third example compares freedom from ignorance to clouds before the sun. Ignorance doesn't exactly take the same form as other types of emotional instability. It isn't a violent feeling one has with anger or desire. It is more like an undertone, like something that's there all the time. Living in ignorance also doesn't bring much obvious suffering. Similarly, when clouds obscure the sun, the sun cannot perform its function of making flowers grow and crops ripen. In the same way, when one is obscured by ignorance, the light of prajñā and jñāna cannot shine and these qualities cannot develop to their fullness. When someone, however, is liberated from ignorance, the light of jñāna can dispel the darkness that surrounds him and can radiate to all beings. This is why the great sun of Buddhahood can dispel the darkness of ignorance of all beings.

The emotionally tainted obscurations are listed in the Abhidharma as the ten basic and twenty secondary defilements. These are even further divided into the obscurations that can be removed by insight and those that can removed by cultivation of insight. But they can also be summarized into the three poisons corresponding to the three examples just given. Sometimes these are also explained in terms of five poisons: attachment, aggression, and ignorance plus pride and jealousy. Jealousy, however, has the same nature as aggression; and pride is rooted in ignorance because it is the belief that one is more gifted or intelligent than other persons. So once these poisons have been removed, all the qualities of Buddhahood can manifest.

This detailed explanation of the freedom from the cognitive obscurations gives nine examples. First, Buddhahood freed from the impurities is compared to the body of Buddha, because there is nothing else that could be used since the Buddha is matchless.

[182] Second, it is compared to honey because once Buddhahood has been achieved, it is capable of giving the taste of perfect dharma to all beings by providing them happiness.

Third, it is compared to a grain freed from the husk because once all the qualities are freed from the husk of ignorance, they can be tasted in all their goodness.

[183] In the next three examples, Buddhahood is compared to gold, a great treasure, and a tree. Buddhahood has a very pure nature since all the fleeting impurities have been removed and it is adorned by myriads of qualities. Because it has a wealth of qualities, it can remove the poverty of all who are stuck in conditioned existence and who suffer from lack of intelligence, lack of faith, and lack of happiness. It can dispel the poverty of other beings by turning the wheel of dharma. Turning the wheel of dharma is not just short-term help; it's a way to achieve ultimate happiness through complete liberation. Buddhahood is

compared to gold because of its natural purity. Because it dispels the poverty of all beings, it is compared to a great treasure. Because it will lead to perfect fruition, it is compared to a tree that grew out from a fruit.

[184] The last three examples show how Buddhahood, freed from the cognitive obscurations, has the nature of the three kāyas. The dharmakāya is compared to a jewel because it is not made up of any other elements. It is also not of an illusory nature so it is compared to a statue made of precious substances.

The sambhogakāya is compared to the king of all beings (Cakravartin) in the womb of a poor and ugly mother. The sambhogakāya here is said to be the lord of all beings on earth. The sambhogakāya can help, protect, and look after all beings.

Finally, the nirmāṇakāya is compared to a precious statue inside its clay cast. It is compared to a very precious statue because it has a special quality of being like a wish-fulfilling gem.[6] When the Buddha appears in the world, the happiness of beings increases. So that is why it is compared here to a statue made of very precious substances, like the wish-fulfilling gem.

These nine examples are of Buddhahood freed from all the cognitive obscurations. Each set of three examples has a specific meaning also. The first three examples—of the Buddha liberated from the lotus, the honey taken from bees, and a kernel removed from its husk—illustrate the fruition of Buddhahood once the cognitive obscurations have been removed. Removing just the emotional

6 Rinpoche says that in previous times when karma was much better, the wish-fulfilling gem was an actual object which would produce what one desired.

obscurations allows one to reach the state of arhats, śrāvakas, or pratyekabuddhas, but one doesn't reach final Buddhahood. Cognitive obscurations must also be removed to attain Buddhahood. At enlightenment all the qualities of body, speech, and mind of the Buddha manifest. The body aspect manifests as in the example of when the Buddha is liberated from the lotus. His speech manifests when he begins giving the taste of the honey of dharma to beings. His mind aspect manifests when the very essence, the kernel, is liberated from the husk.

The last three examples illustrate the ultimate realization which manifests in the form of the three kāyas of the Buddha using the examples of gold, the treasure, and the great tree. Gold is naturally pure, a treasure is naturally plentiful, and a tree is the full manifestation of the fruit. So these are compared to Buddhahood which is the complete liberation from all obscurations.

### *4. Function of Enlightenment*

[185] There are four qualities associated with the function of Buddhahood. It is not tainted by any defilements or remaining mental imprints. Second, it is all-embracing, which is connected to the knowledge aspect of Buddhahood. Third, it is indestructible, which is connected with the uncreated nature of Buddhahood. Fourth, it is the ground of everything. The first three refer to value for one's self and the fourth to value for others.

The first attribute of indestructibility is explained in four ways. It is indestructible because it has no old age, sickness, birth, or death. Being free from old age, it is eternal; being free from sickness, it is at peace; being free from birth, it is permanent; being free from death, it is immortal. The fourth attribute of Buddhahood being the ground of everything is illustrated by the Buddhas being compared to space[7] because its nature is uncreated. Space is just there, it does nothing, but it provides the possibility for everything else to take place. In the same way, the Buddhas provide the space within which all the faculties of the realized ones can be experienced.

[186] The objects of the faculties of the realized ones are experienced in a pure way beyond the four elements. This refers to the pure form kāyas of the Buddha which can be seen by those who are spiritually mature. The ears of the realized ones can hear the pure sounds of the mahāyāna dharma. Their olfactory senses can smell the very pure fragrance of the Buddha's perfect conduct. Their tongue can taste the flavor of the true dharma, really tasting its meaning. Because they've acquired great mastery of samādhi meditation, they can control their meditation and it brings them great bliss. This experience of bliss represents the pure experience of touch. They also have a mental experience of the true nature of everything. This is how the realized ones experience all sensations as pure.

[187] In the ultimate sense, the tathāgatas are like space —space is void and at the same time it provides the possibility for everything to take place in it. The Buddhas are compared to space because of its uncreated and unchanging quality. In the same way, the Buddhas are uncreated and spontaneously present without any effort on their part. Their activity takes place to help other beings

7 Although translated as "space" this refers to the element of ether which is the substance which pervades everything in Aristolian mechanics.

without any reason and they do not think in terms of having to help and doing something to help. The whole thing takes place spontaneously.

[188] These four points will be explained in detail in three parts. The first part is an explanation of how twofold value is achieved by means of the jñāna of how-it-is and of variety. While bodhisattvas are practicing on the path, there is a gradual progression of the manifestation of the two jñānas. In meditation nonconceptual jñāna is present trying to understand the ultimate nature of phenomena. In post-meditation analytical jñāna examines the variety of phenomena to understand its particularities. When these two jñānas are fully developed, they express themselves in the form of the two kāyas of the Buddha which is actually part of the dharmakāya. One is known as the *vimuktikāya* which means the "embodiment of liberation." The other is the dharmakāya or "embodiment of dharma." The vimuktikāya is attained from nonconceptual jñāna which eliminates all obscurations.

The second jñāna is full realization of phenomena representing the clarity aspect of Buddhahood embodied by the dharmakāya. The dharmakāya is obtained as a result of the jñāna of post-meditation. It is the analytical aspect of understanding of phenomena which finds its expression in the dharmakāya at fruition.

So enlightenment is divided into the vimuktikāya and the dharmakāya with the vimuktikāya representing the untainted qualities and the dharmakāya representing the qualities of all-pervasiveness because the dharmakāya pervades all phenomena. These kāyas also have the quality of being uncreated and being indestructible in common.

These three qualities of not tainted, all-embracing, and indestructible represent perfect fulfillment for oneself and have the power to achieve perfect fulfillment for others which is the fourth quality, the happiness of other beings. So the vimuktikāya and dharmakāya represent fulfillment for oneself and perfect fulfillment for others, insofar as they are the ground for all other qualities.

[189] When the defilements have been totally relinquished, Buddhahood becomes perfect fulfillment and all the very fine mental imprints have been totally removed. This contrasts to the śrāvakas or pratyekabuddhas because their mental imprints have not been removed. But all of these disappear completely and the quality of purity is represented by untaintedness.

[190] The second aspect of perfect realization represented by the dharmakāya is the all-pervading quality of jñāna. Once all obscurations have been removed, the buddha jñāna can pervade everything and is not hindered by misperceptions.

[191] The qualities of perfect purity and perfect realization represent untaintedness and all-pervasiveness respectively. Together they have the common quality of being indestructible. This indestructibility, already mentioned, has the characteristics of being eternal, at peace, permanent, and deathless.

[192] Enlightenment has the quality of indestructibility which is not shared by phenomena. Everything which is of a created or composite in nature undergoes aging, sickness, birth, and death. Destructibility manifests as decay corresponding to old age, drastic change corresponds to sickness, interruption corresponds to birth, in the form of the inconceivable change corresponds to death.

[193] The quality of stainless intelligence is the ground for benefiting other beings because it is the basis of all virtuous qualities. Stainless intelligence is the buddha essence once all impurities have been removed and one's knowledge is fully developed. So at this point stainless intelligence is the ground of all qualities for all beings. The function of a person's capabilities and gifts is to provide him or her with the opportunity to do virtuous actions. Therefore buddha nature is the basis of all virtuous qualities.

[194] For example, space is not the cause of form, sound, smell, taste, touch, or mental objects. It doesn't create them, but it provides the environment within which all these things can manifest so forms can be seen, sounds can be heard, etc. In the same way, when disciples practice the path of junction, they get to see the two kāyas of the Buddha, (the vimuktikāya and the dharmakāya) without any obstruction.

### 5. *Endowments*

[196] Buddhahood is inconceivable because it can only be understood by self-cognition jñāna; it is permanent because it has no birth; it is eternal because it is free from aging; it is at peace because it is free from all the changes caused by sickness; it is changeless because it has no death; it is perfectly at peace because it is completely free from the karmic result of suffering; it is all-embracing because of the knowledge of variety; it is free from concept because of the knowledge of how-it-is; it is uninvolved because it is free from the emotional obscurations; it is completely unhindered because it is free from cognitive

obscuration; it is free from coarse sensations because it is in the true sphere of meditation; it is invisible because it has no form; it is imperceptible because it has no characteristics; it is pure because by nature it is totally pure; and it is immaculate because it is free from all incidental stains.

[197] There are 15 qualities of Buddhahood which manifest in the vimuktikāya and the dharmakāya. The Tibetan word for "Buddha" is *sang gay* with *sang* meaning "awakened from the sleep of ignorance," and *gay* meaning "fully blossomed." This shows the two facets of Buddhahood which are purity and realization. These can also be found in the Tibetan words for "enlightenment" which is made up of the two syllables *chang* meaning "purified" and *chub* meaning "assimilated," or "taken in" or "internalized." The first syllable shows the facet of enlightenment, of the complete liberation from all stains and this represents the vimuktikāya aspect. The second syllable refers to the realization aspect of Buddhahood, represented by the dharmakāya. The vimuktikāya and dharmakāya are of value for oneself and value for others respectively. In more detail:

[198] The first quality of enlightenment is inconceivability which is explained first because it is the main quality that runs through all the other qualities of a Buddha. The true qualities of a Buddha cannot be really understood by anyone other than the Buddha himself. Other beings may have an idea of what Buddhahood is, but only a Buddha knows Buddhahood directly.

[199] Enlightenment cannot be understood by means of the three prajñās of study, reflection, and meditation. This is true for ordinary beings all the way up to bodhisattvas of

the tenth level. Enlightenment is beyond this because it is far too subtle to be within the scope of study. When one studies, one can only obtain a very general and indirect knowledge of enlightenment. This is analogous to when one sees a form or hears a sound one apprehends them in a rather gross way since one cannot perceive them directly. Enlightenment cannot be the object of reflection either. When one reflects on something using discursive thought, the object can only be crude and one cannot know the actual nature of the object. So reflection cannot apply to something as subtle as enlightenment because enlightenment is within the realm of the ultimate. Finally, enlightenment cannot be the object of meditation of ordinary beings. However, the prajñā in the meditation of a bodhisattva could understand enlightenment. This knowledge could be called prajñā, but it is more like jñāna. It is the jñāna that manifests more and more in the development of a bodhisattva. It's not so much the result of their meditation as the general process of the unfolding of jñāna.

[200] The inability of ordinary beings to study enlightenment is compared to a blind person. Even though there are visual forms outside, a blind person doesn't have any idea of what it looks like or what it is. In the same way, ordinary beings cannot have an experience of enlightenment. They cannot see, know, or experience the vimuktikāya and the dharmakāya.

Enlightenment is also, in part, inconceivable to deeply realized bodhisattvas who have only a small experience of it. They are compared to a new born baby in a house. If the sun is shining outside and the baby is inside the house, it will get some of the rays of the sun peeping into the house and feel a little bit of the warmth of the sun. In the same way, the realized bodhisattvas have some experience of the buddha qualities as they progress along the bodhisattva levels, but it is a far cry from the full experience of Buddhahood.

[201] The second quality is changelessness which actually covers the second to fifth qualities of permanent, eternal, at peace, and immutable. Enlightenment is changeless because it is present in all beings from the start. It is not created by various causes and conditions so it is permanent. If it never started, then it obviously has no cessation and therefore is eternal. If there's no beginning or no end, then there are no upsetting patterns in the middle. So enlightenment is at peace. There is just nothing to disturb the nature of enlightenment so it is not affected by any kind of change. It is immutable because enlightenment is always at rest and its true nature never changes.

[202] The sixth through the eleventh qualities express the perfect fulfillment of purification and realization. The sixth quality is being perfectly at peace because all suffering has been completely uprooted. This corresponds to the truth of cessation —when all impurities have been removed, there is no longer any opportunity for suffering to arise. If impurities were still present, these would still be caused by emotional disruptions. So Buddhahood is perfectly at peace and free from emotional obscurations.

The seventh quality is all-embracing which relates to clarity from cognitive obscurations. When these obscurations are removed, there is a very clear knowledge of everything. Everything is as clear as though it were in the palm of one's hand.

The eighth quality is being concept-free because enlightenment doesn't dwell on any idea or any concept. The ninth quality is being uninvolved. This could also be translated in the sense of "not stuck to anything." Enlightenment doesn't stick to anything insofar as there is no emotional obscuration to make one cling to something.

[203] The tenth quality is being unhindered. At this point knowledge is totally unhindered because there are no longer any cognitive obscurations. The eleventh quality is freedom from coarse sensatic s which is the ability to meditate without being disturbed by drowsiness or agitation. Drowsiness in meditation provokes a dull state of mind, an absence of clarity. Agitation causes a constant movement of thoughts which prevents good meditation. So at the point of enlightenment, there are no longer any disrupting forces in meditation. Because there is no hindrance, the meditation is free from coarse sensations.

[204] The last four qualities of enlightenment are described in terms of the four qualities of purity. The first quality is invisibility. Buddhahood is formless and therefore invisible. The twelfth quality is imperceptible because Buddhahood has no solid characteristics. The thirteenth is purity which could also be rendered as "wholesomeness," meaning that nothing in it is impure. The last quality is immaculateness because all the impurities that would impede proper meditation have been removed.

### 6. Manifestation of Enlightenment

In the root text, the sixth point is called "manifestation." But literally it means, "going into enlightenment" or "entering enlightenment" so that it means actualizing enlightenment.

[205] First manifestation of enlightenment is the characteristic of being uncreated because is eternal, centerless, and endless. This means that enlightenment doesn't start at a given point and therefore cannot stop at a given point or abide in between these two points.

The second characteristic is indivisibility of emptiness and jñāna. Everything being voidness refers to the *dharmadhātu* quality of everything. The voidness and jñāna cannot exist separately as can, for example, a single rope made by taking white and black thread and braiding them together. They are inseparable by nature with one unable to exist without the other. There is jñāna, but the nature of that jñāna is voidness. There is voidness, but the nature of that voidness is jñāna. In the same way, the voidness itself is jñāna. It has a quality of clarity that's not a blank like the nonexistence of the rabbit's horns. It is very alive, so this voidness creates the possibility for everything to manifest clearly.

The third characteristic is "to be free from the two" which indicates freedom from all extreme notions. This characteristic of right understanding is that one doesn't make any false assumptions or any incorrect denials about it. A false assumption would be to attribute a quality to something that doesn't have that quality. An incorrect denial would be not recognizing a quality, if it really existed. So freedom from the two is to be free from these two distortions of the true nature of things.

The fourth characteristic is freedom from all obscurations or "veils" so there is no longer any emotional obscuration, cognitive obscuration, or obstruction of meditation. When these three have been removed, a quality of stainlessness emerges.

The last characteristic is being beyond thought because enlightenment cannot be understood by discursive thought. Enlightenment is not an outer object so it cannot be understood by discursive thinking. The only way to understand it is by meditation. The supreme yogi (the Buddha) then rests within the nature of the dharmadhātu and in meditation can understand it.

### *Dharmakāya Qualities*

[206] The first four qualities of the dharmakāya represent perfect knowledge. The dharmakāya has qualities which are unfathomable and cannot be understood because of their vastness. The dharmakāya doesn't have any solid reality, therefore it is present everywhere. This unfathomable nature means that there are so many qualities which are so vast and so deep that one cannot even discern what they exactly are. The second quality is being unaccountable. The dharmakāya has so many qualities that one cannot count them precisely. The third quality is inconceivability because the dharmakāya is so deep that one cannot understand it easily. The fourth quality is incomparability because there is nothing else one can compare it to. It cannot be compared to ordinary phenomena because ordinary phenomena are emotionally tainted and it cannot be compared to the fruition of the hīnayāna path. The fifth quality represents the complete purity of Buddhahood. The verse says "the immaculate space of the tathāgatas" which means the dharmakāya is completely free from all obscurations including the very fine traces left behind by those obscurations.

### *Sambhogakāya Qualities*

[207] The sambhogakāya exhibits the deep and vast aspect of dharma. The deep aspect of dharma refers to voidness and the vast aspect refers to the various levels practiced on the path. The sambhogakāya shows the speech aspect with the dharma taking place without interruption. The second quality of the sambhogakāya is the Buddha's body adorned with the 32 marks and 80 signs of beauty which are like a radiant body. This manifests to realized bodhisattvas in this very brilliant, pure form.

The third quality of the Buddha's mind in the sambhogakāya is his mind is always engaged in the goal of helping liberate all beings. This compassionate mind manifests to realized bodhisattvas.

The fourth quality relates to the activity of the sambhogakāya. The acts of the sambhogakāya are compared to a wish-fulfilling jewel which can accomplish anything without thought or effort. Likewise, the deeds of the sambhogakāya are accomplished spontaneously, without any effort.

The fifth quality shows how this activity of the sambhogakāya actually manifests by appearing in many different substantial forms to beings and performing many different kinds of deeds that guide them to liberation. Still while manifesting as substantial forms, it is insubstantial.

### *Nirmāṇakāya Qualities*

[208] The nirmāṇakāya of the Buddha is the origin for liberation of beings in three different stages. In the nirmāṇakāya form, the Buddha causes ordinary beings to enter the path of liberation leading them away from saṃsāra. Once beings have entered the path, the Buddhas

help them to purify the defilements and gain realization. In the third stage if someone has developed fully on the path, the nirmāṇakāya will predict when a person will become a Buddha and in which buddha field he or she will go and what his or her name will be.

The nirmāṇakāya of the Buddha is always present in our world. The nirmāṇakāya is not permanent in nature, but a permanence of continuity of buddha activity. A Buddha enters our world and then he passes away and one could think that Buddha activity then stops. But this is not the case because once a Buddha has passed away, another Buddha comes along continuing the buddha activity. The spontaneous presence of buddha activity in our world can be compared to the way in which the form realms abide in space. In the same way, buddha activity is always present in our world.

[209] Enlightenment takes three different aspects; through the dharmakāya, the sambhogakāya, and the nirmāṇakāya which can be described in terms of seven names. First, enlightenment is called "spontaneously present" because it does not rely on anything else depending entirely on the presence of the buddha essence within us. The second name is "all-knowing" or "omniscient" which refers to perfect knowledge of the Buddha. The third name is "Buddhahood" which comes from the word dharmakāya and covers both the quality of complete purity and full knowledge. The fourth name is "supreme nirvāṇa" with the word "supreme" added to "nirvāṇa" because nirvāṇa is beyond suffering. The arhats also believe that they go beyond suffering so the word "supreme" is added to show going beyond this suffering. The fifth name is "inconceivability" because enlightenment

is not the object of intellectual speculation and can only be understood through the deepest aspect of understanding, prajñā. The sixth name is "victory over the enemy" in which saṃsāra is compared to the enemy and Buddhahood is the complete victory over that enemy. The seventh is "self-cognisant nature" because Buddhahood is the object of the realization of the self-cognisant jñāna. So it is the nature that knows itself.

[210] Enlightenment also has three aspects: an aspect of depth which relates to the dharmakāya because it is very difficult to understand; an aspect of vastness which relates to sambhogakāya insofar as it has great powers to help beings; and an aspect of greatness of nature which refers to the nirmāṇakāya and its quality of infinite compassion which allows the nirmāṇakāya to act in all the different ways according to a being's karma and capabilities.

### *The Svābhāvikakāya*

[211] The svābhāvikakāya of the dharmakāya has five intrinsic characteristics and five qualities.

The first characteristic is uncreated. The dharmakāya is uncreated because it has no beginning, no abiding, and no end. It is also the indivisible union of the untainted dharmadhātu and the perfectly completed jñāna. This dharmadhātu means the voidness aspect of the true nature which is completely free from the four extremes and the eight mental fabrications. This voidness is explained in the second turning of the wheel of dharma. In the relative sense everything appears, but ultimately everything is of a void nature. This corresponds to the teachings on the presence of the buddha essence in the mind of all beings that were given in the third turning. So the dharmadhātu and jñāna are perfectly united.

The second characteristic of the dharmakāya is being completely free from the two extreme notions of trying to add to it something that is not there or trying to remove something that doesn't need to be removed. So it is just as it is. When practicing on the path, it is within this nature that one has to rest the mind in meditation and one has to recognize the jñāna of insight. At the beginning one learns theoretically that the true nature of existence is the indivisibility of voidness and clarity. Then one gains a definite conviction that it is true and allows oneself to be immersed within that true nature in meditation. The third characteristic is being completely free from emotional and cognitive obscurations and free from the obscuration that prevents one from meditating properly.

[213] The fourth characteristic is being free of the obscurations so the svābhāvikakāya is flawless. The fifth characteristic is clarity. Because the dharmakāya is stainless, it is not the object of intellectual speculation but the object of cognition of the supreme yogis who abide continually in the union of prajñā and skillful means (Skt. *upāya*). It is also clarity because the dharmadhātu is itself by nature completely pure.

[214] There are five outward characteristics of the svābhāvikakāya. The first quality is immeasurability because it cannot be fathomed in any way. It is not like an ordinary composite object which can investigated in regard to its color, form, and different attributes. The second quality is uncountability. If one takes any ordinary object, one can count it, but this is impossible for the svābhāvikakāya. The third quality is inconceivability. All

ordinary objects can be intellectually worked with because they have form, sound, shape, taste, and so on but the svābhāvikakāya is free from the four extremes and the eight conceptual fabrications. However, this svābhāvikakāya is not totally blank because its great clarity can be apprehended by the yogi who can understand it through his self-cognisant jñāna. The fifth quality is ultimate purity in which all the subtle traces of the emotional, cognitive, and meditative obscurations have been removed.

[215] There are five reasons for these qualities. The svābhāvikakāya is immeasurable because there is no way in which it can be reckoned by ordinary means because of its great vastness. It is uncountable because there is nothing solid to account for. It is completely immeasurable since it is beyond the four extremes and the eight conceptual fabrications. It is inconceivable because if we try to examine it by discursive thought, it cannot be apprehended because it doesn't have the characteristics of ordinary objects. It also cannot be understood in terms of existing or not existing and that is why an ordinary beings cannot grasp the svābhāvikakāya. It is incomparable because the Buddha has qualities which are not shared by anyone else. Finally, it is the ultimate purity and because it lacks even the very fine mental traces of obscurations.

### *The Sambhogakāya*

[216] In general, the Buddha has two form kāyas: one which is the ultimate form kāya, the sambhogakāya, which manifests to those bodhisattvas with very pure karma. This is not because the Buddha has the thought, "This person can see me because he is good." It is just a function of the

way in which beings perceive the forms of the Buddha. Beings who are quite pure can perceive the sambhogakāya. Beings who are less pure can perceive only the nirmāṇa-kāya form. This can be illustrated by an example of the reflection of the moon in water. If the moon reflects in a very clear pond, the image of the moon is very clear. If it reflects in very dirty water, the image of the moon is less clear. In the same way, bodhisattvas on the ten levels are quite pure, so they can perceive the sambhogakāya form of the Buddha. Beings who are less pure can only perceive the nirmāṇakāya, even though the buddha activity is going on all the time. When beings are not ready, the Buddha will teach them a simpler way of looking at things to lead them gradually to the understanding of the real truth. But the sambhogakāya level always teaches the absolute meaning of things. The Buddha at this level doesn't need to use examples or simplified explanations because he manifests to beings who are already realized. So the first quality of the sambhogakāya is speech which expresses all the aspects of the dharma at all times.

The second quality of the sambhogakāya is a body in which the activity of the Buddha is unceasing and manifests through many different emanations. The sambhogakāya represents the emanations which are very faithful to the nature of the dharmakāya itself. In the example of the reflection of the moon in water, the sambhogakāya form makes a very faithful reflection of the qualities of the dharmakāya. So it is said the qualities of the body of the sambhogakāya manifest the real qualities of the dharmakāya.

The third quality of the sambhogakāya is mind which is the pure compassion of the Buddha, so that the natural outflow of this compassion is unceasing help to all beings.

From the dharmakāya's compassion springs the sambhogakāya, and the sambhogakāya is the source of buddha activity. Even the activity of the nirmāṇakāya springs from the compassion of the sambhogakāya which is the expression of the compassion of the dharmakāya.

[217] The fourth quality of the sambhogakāya is that of the Buddha's activity. The activity of the sambhogakāya is completely spontaneous and does not need any thought to take place and entirely satisfies all the wishes of beings. The fifth quality of the sambhogakāya is manifesting something which is not really its true nature, like the wish-fulfilling gem. If one puts a gem against a background of one color it will manifest that color, although that color is not the gem's nature. In the same way, the sambhogakāya manifests in a miraculous way of appearing which is not its real nature, because the sambhogakāya is never divorced from the dharmakāya—it is forever abiding in the dharmakāya.

[218] The sambhogakāya has five different aspects. The first is uninterrupted speech, of continually giving very deep and vast teachings to the pure disciples.

The second is the quality of emanating of body without interruption. The sambhogakāya manifests the true qualities of enlightenment to the realized bodhisattvas. What the realized bodhisattvas see is a form which is adorned with all the marks and signs of a Buddha.

The third quality is the mind of the sambhogakāya that is constantly engaged in activity to help beings as the result of its pure nonconceptual compassion. This compassion helps pure beings, so buddha activity is not aimed only at impure beings.

The fourth quality of the sambhogakāya is that it is

constantly acting spontaneously with its body, speech, and mind. The sambhogakāya body is constantly manifesting physically, and the mind is continually acting to help pure beings, and the speech is constantly giving teachings all without thinking about it.

The fifth quality is being able to manifest beyond its true nature. The sambhogakāya shows itself in forms that correspond to the spiritual maturity of beings. For pure beings it emanates in the form of the sambhogakāya; for impure beings it shows itself in the form of the nirmāṇakāya. It displays visible forms, but these are not its actual nature because its actual nature is the dharmakāya.

[219] For example, a jewel may give off different colors due to the background colors, but itself has no such colors. The jewel does not have a nature of being white, yellow, blue etc. but because it is very transparent, the colors of the background can be seen in the jewel. In the same way, enlightenment can manifest in different forms due to the various circumstances created by beings. The dharmakāya itself doesn't change, but reflects all the various conditions of beings in the way it manifests to them.

### *Nirmāṇakāya*

[220] The nirmāṇakāya referred to here is the supreme nirmāṇakāya which is the historical Buddha with 32 marks and the 80 signs on his body and 60 different qualities of speech. This is the form of the Buddha we know as the Buddha Śākyamuni, and the Buddha Maitreya who will manifest in the future. The nirmāṇakāya is represented by the one thousand Buddhas that will come in this present world cycle. All these Buddhas will show various deeds to

help beings. The Śākyamuni Buddha performed 12 main deeds on the path to liberation.

The ground of buddha activity is the dharmakāya. The sambhogakāya and the nirmāṇakāya manifest to help beings, emanating from the dharmakāya without any change and without being separate from the dharmakāya. The Buddha sees all worlds just as they are and with his compassion he perceives the suffering of beings. The Buddha knows that if these beings practice, they will achieve enlightenment because all beings are endowed with buddha essence. So having seen the world through his great compassion and having seen the need to help beings without departing from the dharmakāya, the Buddha helps them through the form kāyas.

### *Twelve Deeds of the Buddha*

First the Buddha took birth as a god in a paradise called Tuṣita which is a place of great happiness. When he was in Tuṣita, he taught the dharma to the gods. Although this was the first deed of the Buddha, it is not counted as one of the twelve deeds because the twelve deeds refer to activities in our world. Before he left Tuṣita, he appointed the bodhisattva Maitreya as the representative of the Buddhas in Tuṣita empowering him to give teachings there.

Before the Buddha came into our world, he actually had five visions. He saw his mother, the place of his birth, the time, and the kind of people he would be associated with in his life. He saw his caste as a royal family because if he had been born in a low caste he would have automatically been cut off from most persons. The previous buddha, Buddha Kāśyapa, was born in a Brahmin family for a similar reason because at the time the Brahmins had the greatest prestige. Buddha Śākyamuni was born into a royal family because the royal caste had the greatest prestige at the time. Then he saw his mother who was worthy of bearing a Buddha with all his perfect marks and signs inside her womb. He also saw that the beings associated with him lived in India, so India would be the right place for him to manifest. He also saw the right time to manifest which was about 500 B.C. because beings were spiritually ready for his coming. He saw the country in which he should go because there he would be able to help beings the most. Having foreseen these five things, the Buddha left Tuṣita and entered our world.

[221] The second deed was to enter the womb of his mother and his mother perceived this in the form of a white elephant with six tusks entering her womb. The third deed was to take birth in a normal way (his mother's womb). Actually, the Buddha had the power to be born in any way—he could have appeared miraculously from a lotus or just appeared from the sky, but he chose to manifest in a normal birth because all the beings he had to relate to, including his disciples, were born from the womb. Had he had a miraculous birth, they might have thought, "Oh, we are not like him because he has just fallen from space and can do all these things, but we can't do them because we are just ordinary people." So he took a normal birth to show that he was sharing the conditions of all humans.

The fourth deed was that he became very proficient in all arts and crafts. When the Buddha was a little boy, he learned the different aspects of knowledge. He learned to write in the sixty different languages, learned all the different skills, the martial arts, and all the aspects of knowledge. He became extremely proficient and skilled in all of them. The reason he did all this was that later when he was going to teach, there would be no risk of people saying, "Well, he is teaching all these things involving the spiritual life because he was a failure in worldly things."

[222] The fifth deed was that he enjoyed the company of his wife and consorts in his father's palace. This was to eliminate the belief that the Buddha was so extraordinary because he didn't know what pleasure was all about. To offset this belief he showed that he could indeed enjoy the pleasures of the world. Later he showed that there is no need to become involved with these pleasures and cling to them, because they are futile pleasures because as they do not last forever. Instead one should practice the way to liberation without attachment.

The sixth and seventh deeds were to eliminate the extreme of overindulgence of pleasures and enjoyment without caring for anything else and the extreme of practicing too many hardships thinking that this will bring liberation. To show the pointlessness of these extremes, the Buddha renounced the world. At the time the Buddha had been living with all the pleasures of his palace with his wife and consorts. To show this was too much of a fetter, he secretly fled from the palace at night, cut his hair off, and took up the life of a ascetic. Once he left the palace and found a teacher, he practiced extreme austerities by the banks of a river for six years. This was to demonstrate that practicing austerities was not the way to achieve realization. Instead, the final realization is the understanding of the true nature of the mind.

The eighth deed was to go to Bodhgaya (in India) which is known as "the heart of enlightenment." This is the place where the one thousand Buddhas of this time cycle will go to reach enlightenment. His ninth deed was to vanquish the host of māra which are demons. The true meaning of this is that through his varja-like samādhi the Buddha became victorious over all the defilements that were known as the demon of the aggregates, the demon of defilements and so on. These demons or obstacles appeared in front of him to stop him from reaching Buddhahood. They tried to stop him through attachment, aggression, and ignorance. For attachment, the demons created a very beautiful woman who tried to tempt the Buddha, but he overcame this. Then they tried to delude him by producing a messenger who said that his father had died and Devadatta, who was an enemy of the Buddha, was going to take over the kingdom. They also tried to arouse his anger by producing a tremendous army of demons who tried to attack the Buddha through their amazing displays of negative miracles. But the whole time, the Buddha just remained in meditation and was immersed in a state of loving kindness unswayed by desire, anger, or delusion. As a result he demonstrated the tenth deed which was to achieve perfect enlightenment.

[223] Having achieved enlightenment, the Buddha performed the eleventh deed which was turning the wheel of dharma. The first turning taught the four noble truths which was to help the disciples of hīnayāna. The second turning was the teaching of voidness and the original nature of everything, of dharmadhātu. The third turning was the teachings on the clarity aspect of jñāna that showed that the true nature of everything is the union of clarity and voidness and was intended for bodhisattvas who could reach enlightenment.

The twelfth deed of the Buddha was his passing away. The buddha could see that if he remained among human beings all the time, they wouldn't really develop a sense of renunciation. To kindle a weariness of saṃsāra and develop a wish for liberation in beings, the Buddha appeared to die.

### *Progressive Training*

[224] The first way the Buddha helped in the nirmāṇakāya was the 12 deeds. The second way was through helping beings reach liberation or "ripening" them. For ordinary beings, the Buddha helps them enter the hīnayāna by guiding them in the understanding of that path. When beings are more spiritually developed, he guides them into the mahāyāna and helps them relinquish their emotional and cognitive obscurations until they reach enlightenment.

The Buddha helps beings, including those who have not yet had any contact with the Buddha's teachings, enter the hīnayāna path by teaching the relative truth because the ultimate truth is quite difficult to understand at first. He teaches that all composite phenomena are impermanent and that everything that is tainted by emotional impurities automatically implies suffering. Then he taught that all these conditions and tainted phenomena are devoid of any self and that this subject that seems to be apprehending phenomena is itself not real. So in effect, beings are taught the three characteristics of saṃsāra; impermanence, suffering, and self.

Once beings understand impermanence and suffering, they will want to eliminate these. Once they understand there is no "self," they will want to relinquish this illusion and understand it. So the teaching of non-self has the benefit of making beings want to go beyond suffering, impermanence, and a mistaken belief in a self, and making them want to reach nirvāṇa. So the benefit of these teachings is that they bring beings onto the path in the immediate future and help them liberate themselves from saṃsāra to achieve a state of peace in the more distant future.

[225] The second turning and the bodhisattva path teachings are given to those beings who have already entered the path to peace, but mistakenly believe that they have already achieved nirvāṇa. So teachings such as the *Lotus Sūtra* (*Saddharmauṇḍarīka* sūtra) describe the real nature of phenomena and teach that they have not achieved final enlightenment and to reach this final enlightenment, they have to practice two qualities. They have to develop prajñā which leads them to understand that they must go beyond conditioned existence. Simultaneously, they must develop the true compassion unsupported by any concepts. This makes them want to go beyond peace just for oneself. So these beings who have achieved peace for themselves are taught they must go on to perfect enlightenment.

[226] Through these teachings practitioners of the hīnayāna are brought into the fold of the mahāyāna. They will undergo a change of motivation and acquire real prajñā. They will understand the nonexistence of a personal self and the non-existence of phenomena. Through these changes, they will cultivate the skillful means of compassion (the emptiness) united with deeper understanding (prajñā).

The immediate result of these teachings of the nirmāṇakāya leads beings onto the path to peace and brings them into the fold of the hīnayāna. After that, the Buddha gives them the absolute meaning of the teachings and places them onto the mahāyāna path.

The third aspect of buddha activity is enlightenment. When beings have reached the pure eighth, ninth, and tenth bodhisattva levels, the Buddha makes a prediction of their future enlightenment. He will say, "Later on in such and such a time cycle (Skt. *kalpa*), you will become a Buddha with the name of so and so, and have disciples by the names of so and so, your teachings will endure for such and such duration of time, and your buddha field will be called such and such."

### *How the Kāyas are Grouped*

[227] The kāyas of the Buddha are the dharmakāya, sambhogakāya, and the nirmāṇakāya. The dharmakāya is the most difficult to understand because it is beyond the four extremes and the eight mental fabrications.

The sambhogakāya has the quality of great power. The nirmāṇakāya, on the other hand, expresses itself with respect to what beings need. When the nirmāṇakāya manifests in a given place, all the beings who live in that place won't necessarily enter the dharma. However, when the sambhogakāya teaches in a given buddha field, all the beings there enter the dharma because they are already very close to the final realization. The sambhogakāya, in effect, teaches the final realization and is extremely powerful because it talks continually about the absolute meaning of things.

The nirmāṇakāya expresses the teachings in a way that beings can relate to it and teaches more relative than absolute meaning. This is why the nirmāṇakāya appears in forms that are actual experiences of beings.

[228] To summarize, the dharmakāya is the depth, the very expression of the dharmadhātu. The sambhogakāya

represents the vastness of buddha activity which is all-powerful. And the nirmāṇakāya represents greatness of nature which means it has great compassion that makes it possible for buddha activity to express itself in ways beings can relate to. The buddha kāyas can also be divided into the dharmakāya which expresses the true nature of things and the other two form kāyas. The sambhogakāya and the nirmāṇakāya are called the form kāyas because they are the ones people can actually see and relate to. However, these two form kāyas are always present in the dharmakāya in the same way that visible objects are present in space.

### *7. Permanence*

[229] The very nature of enlightenment is changeless, immutable and will be explained using ten different reasons —seven for the form kāyas and three for the dharmakāya. The dharmakāya has the permanence of nature, the sambhogakāya the permanence of continuity, and the nirmāṇakāya the permanence of uninterruptedness. The first reason for permanence of the kāyas is due to endless conditions which means that Buddhahood can be achieved through a combination of many different causes. One condition for realizing Buddhahood is the accumulation of virtue by practicing the six pāramitās. The other condition is the accumulation of insight which is done through meditation. When these two accumulations have been completed the two form kāyas will manifest as the result of these endless causes and will be able to manifest permanently to all different beings: the sambhogakāya with its permanence of continuity and the nirmāṇakāya with its permanence of being uninterupted.

The second reason for the permanence of the kāyas is the inexhaustible number of beings and buddha activity will be around as long as there are beings. However, the number of beings is so inexhaustible that the form kāyas will always have to manifest in order to help them. If one being has been liberated, there are still many, many other beings to liberate.

The third reason for the permanence of the form kāyas is the great compassionate love of the Buddha. If the Buddhas weren't continually inspired by compassion, their activity would stop. However, the Buddhas have non-referential compassion so their activity goes on all the time as a mother always has love for her only son.

The fourth reason is miraculous cause. Even if the Buddhas had compassion, if they didn't have the power to make this activity possible, then it wouldn't take place. But the Buddhas have miraculous powers so that they can continually help with whatever is necessary for the good of beings. The fifth reason for the permanence of the form kāyas is that the Buddhas have realized the sameness of saṃsāra and nirvāṇa and do not see themselves defiled and polluted by saṃsāra when helping beings in saṃsāra. The sixth reason is that they possess the untainted happiness. And the seventh reason is that they have mastery over all qualities.

The next three reasons express the permanence of the dharmakāya. The dharmakāya is permanent because the evil of death has been vanquished. Ninth is that the dharmakāya has no material essence. It is not of a conditioned nature, therefore it is permanent. The tenth reason is that the dharmakāya is the protector of the world and pervades everything. In more detail:

[230] The first four reasons for explaining how the form kāyas are constantly present in saṃsāra and the last three reasons explain how they do not forsake saṃsāra.

To begin, the form kāyas are always present in saṃsāra because the bodhisattvas hold the true dharma, having devoted their bodies, lives, and resources to this for aeons. The form kāyas manifest due to endless causes which are all the virtuous actions done by the bodhisattvas for endless aeons.

The second reason for permanence is that the Buddhas act for the benefit of all beings. They do not work for just their own countrymen, relatives, or disciples because when they began on the mahāyāna path, they took a vow to reach enlightenment for the sake of all beings.

[231] Since there is an inexhaustible number of beings to be liberated from saṃsāra, the form kāyas are permanent. However, if the Buddhas didn't have compassion, this activity would stop at a certain point. Inspired by this compassion, they are constantly helping beings so that they manifest continuously. Fourth, even if the Buddhas were willing to help, if they did not have the power to help, no buddha activity could take place. The Buddhas, however, possess full miraculous powers so that they can help beings in whatever way needed.

[232] The form kāyas are permanent because the Buddhas do not forsake saṃsāra for three reasons. If the Buddhas saw saṃsāra as bad and nirvāṇa as good, they would be inclined to give up saṃsāra and achieve nirvāṇa. This would be an obstacle to the accomplishment of buddha activity to help other beings. However, they possess perfect knowledge so they understand the inseparability of nirvāṇa and saṃsāra and therefore

manifest continually in saṃsāra to help beings. The Buddhas also do not forsake the world because they possess the supreme bliss of samādhi. Even though the Buddhas could see the inseparability of saṃsāra and nirvāṇa, if they had to undergo terrible sufferings in saṃsāra, after a time they wouldn't be able to bear it. However, instead they experience the supreme bliss of meditation (samādhi).

[233] If the Buddhas saw the inseparability of saṃsāra and nirvāṇa but still had karma and obscuration, then from time to time they would experience the suffering of saṃsāra again. This would become an obstacle to their helping beings and would eventually render them powerless. So the third reason that the form kāyas are permanent is that since they are not polluted by worldly impurities, they can remain permanently in the world to help beings.

The first of four reasons that the dharmakāya is permanent is that it is immortal. In saṃsāra, one has to experience birth which implies sickness, old age, and death. But in Buddhahood there is no longer any death because the causes of death have been removed. The Buddhas have totally eradicated all obscurations which frees them from karma and therefore places them beyond the reach of death.

[234] Secondly, the nature of dharmakāya is uncreated. From the beginning of time Buddhahood was free from birth, old age, sickness, and death. The Buddhas have realized this uncreated true nature by perceiving it as it is and made it manifest just as it is. This nature is perfectly at peace and beyond all conditioned phenomena. This original uncreatedness of the true nature is manifested in

Buddhahood and that is why Buddhahood is permanent.

The third reason is Buddhahood constitutes a permanent refuge for those who are without help. Why is this? Beings are subject to impermanence, suffering, and dangers; but when the ultimate realization is achieved all these characteristics vanish. So the one who embodies freedom from impermanence becomes the protection for all beings who are still subjected to change.

[235] The form kāyas do not have the same permanence of nature. As their name indicates they take form and as soon as there is form there is no longer the characteristic of uncreatedness. So they are not permanent in nature and are not free from impermanence. However, the sambhogakāya has the permanence of uninterruptedness because it has the five definite characteristics which it manifests so the buddha field where the sambhogakāya is manifesting can never change. And the sambhogakāya itself never passes away, so it has the permanence of unceasingness.

The nirmāṇakāya has the permanence of continuity. A Buddha comes and gives his teaching and then passes away, but his or her buddha activity doesn't stop. This nirmāṇakāya form will begin in another place so that buddha activity is going on continually.

### 8. *Inconceivability of Enlightenment*

[236] Enlightenment is inconceivable for six reasons. First, it is inconceivable because it is ineffable which means that the qualities of enlightenment cannot be described in words. Second, it is the ultimate truth. The Tibetan word for "relative truth" or reality is *kunzop*. The syllable *kun* means "all," and indicates that these objects

can be apprehended by all (rather than just extraordinary) beings. The second syllable *zop* means "false." Everyone perceives these things in a false way. Enlightenment consists of the ultimate truth which is the absolute truth or the way things truly are. Third, it is not the object of intellectual investigation because it is beyond the four extremes and eight conceptual fabrications. Fourth, it is beyond comparisons so one cannot find any examples to describe it. Fifth, it is peerless, being the highest possible quality so that one cannot find anything with which to compare it with. Sixth, it is neither conditioned existence nor the peace of the arhats. In more detail:

[237] Enlightenment is inconceivable because it is ineffable. "Ineffable" means that it cannot be expressed in words. Ordinary objects of the relative world, say a pillar or a bowl, one can describe it in words. If an object can be represented by words, it can also be conceived by mind. However, Buddhahood cannot be described by words so it cannot be fully understood by mind. It is ineffable because it is the ultimate truth. All ordinary objects have sound, taste, smell, etc. and can be apprehended by means of names, symbols, and descriptions of existence and so on. Enlightenment, however, cannot be described in words because it is beyond the four extremes and eight conceptual fabrications. All one can do is to describe what it is not.

Enlightenment is the ultimate truth and it cannot be investigated intellectually. If one wants to investigate an object, one would have to apprehend it intellectually either directly or through deductive reasoning. To investigate intellectually, one has to use reason and to use reason one has to rely on terms of comparison. Since enlightenment is peerless there's nothing that could be compared to it. And if one cannot make any deductions, one cannot make any inferences about enlightenment because it is not comprised of saṃsāra or nirvāṇa. Therefore there is nothing that could compare to it.

[238] Besides these first six reasons of the inconceivability of Buddhahood there are two specific characteristics of Buddhahood. The specific quality of Buddhahood is that it never abides in saṃsāra or in the selfish peace of the arhats. It is nonabiding because it has no concept of the qualities of nirvāṇa or the defects of saṃsāra. The seventh and eighth reason for the inconceivability of enlightenment, therefore, is nonabiding and having no concept of the faults of saṃsāra.

[239] There are five reasons for the inconceivability of the dharmakāya. The dharmakāya is ineffable, it consists of the ultimate truth, it is not the object of intellectual investigation; it is beyond comparisons; and it is peerless. The dharmakāya therefore is extremely subtle, and being so subtle, it cannot be comprehended by mind, ideas, or concepts. The sixth reason is that it is comprised of neither conditioned existence nor selfish peace. There are two more reasons for this: not dwelling in saṃsāra or nirvāṇa and not having any thought of the defects of saṃsāra. Since the seventh and eighth reasons are not part of the object of the phenomena present in any of these levels of existence, they are also not conceivable by mind.

[240] In summary, the Buddhas have unsurpassable qualities: unsurpassable knowledge of their jñāna, unsurpassable compassion which is the power to help. They are beyond all descriptions so Buddhahood which has been described in terms of eight points up to now is, in fact,

beyond all descriptions. The Buddhas are also called the "spontaneously present ones," meaning Buddhahood is not created by anything else or dependent upon something external. They appear by themselves continually and they realize their own Buddhahood. When these spontaneous present ones reach enlightenment, this is the last point on their journey. They begin with making a resolution to reach Buddhahood for the sake of all beings. When they have reached enlightenment, this is also the final point in terms of refuge and the final goal of every being. So this final point of arrival is inconceivable for all beings. Even for bodhisattvas on the tenth level, it is inconceivable. So it is even more inconceivable for bodhisattvas on lower levels, not to mention ordinary beings.

# CHAPTER 9

# *The Qualities of Buddhahood*

### *The Qualities in Terms of the Kāyas*

[241] The qualities of enlightenment will be expressed in terms of the two kāyas with the qualities of value for oneself corresponding to the absolute truth and the dharmakāya and the qualities that are of value for others corresponding to relative truth and the two form kāyas. The qualities of value for oneself are related to the quality of freedom and the qualities of value for others related to the qualities of maturity.

The qualities of freedom can be compared to the sun appearing from behind the clouds. An unobscured sun is free from clouds and not a creation of the clouds because once the clouds have been removed, the sun becomes visible again. In the same way, the twofold jñāna of the Buddha is not the result of cognitive and emotional obscurations because once the jñāna is free from impurities, it manifests as full knowledge of how-it-is and variety.

The qualities of maturity began in the past when the bodhisattva had to gather the accumulation of virtue and the accumulation of insight. Through the practice of these two accumulations all the various qualities matured which gave rise to the form kāyas resulting in the 32 qualities of maturity and 32 qualities of freedom of Buddhahood.

[242] The ground for acquiring fulfillment for oneself is the ultimate kāya in which all thoughts have been eliminated and all the good qualities of Buddhahood have been fully developed. If the ground were only a relative kāya, it would automatically involve impermanence; therefore it could not provide a constant basis for the qualities. The ultimate kāya, however, is unchanging so it can provide the best basis for fulfillment for oneself and others. It is said therefore that the symbol kāyas of the great sages are the ground of the greatest possible good for beings. "Great sages" is a name for the Buddhas. The phrase in Sanskrit is *rishis* meaning someone who is very straight forward, honest, and speaks only the truth. It can be used for nonBuddhists or arhats but in this context it is used for the Buddhas. The phrase "symbol kāyas" mean that the Buddhas express themselves in symbolic form in relative reality for the best value for beings.

[243] The first kāya, the dharmakāya, represents fulfillment for oneself: it has 32 qualities of freedom which include the ten powers, the four fearlessnesses, and the 18 distinctive qualities. They are called qualities of freedom because the dharmakāya is free from all obscurations.

The two form kāyas exist in the relative level of reality and are represented by the qualities of a perfect being. The Buddha manifests in the form kāyas so he can be visible to other beings and adopt the most perfect form of all 32 marks and 80 signs. These marks and signs are the fruition of all the virtue that had been accumulated on the path when the Buddhas were bodhisattvas.

## *The 32 Qualities of Freedom*

[244] The qualities of freedom are compared to different things. The ten powers are compared to a vajra. A vajra cannot be destroyed or defeated by anything else and in the same way, the ten powers of the Buddha can defeat everything else by cutting through all ignorance. The four fearlessnesses of the Buddha are compared to a lion because a lion is naturally intrepid. A lion hasn't any fear because he knows he is the strongest animal in the forest and no other animal would even think of attacking him. In the same way the Buddha is not afraid of anything because he has seen the true nature of everything and will not make a mistake and fear that someone will prove him wrong. The 18 distinctive qualities of the Buddha are compared to space. One can mix the other elements such as earth and water, air and fire, but space cannot be mixed with any other element because it has characteristics different from any of the other elements. In the same way the attributes of the Buddha are distinctive and are not the same as those of other beings.

Finally, the two kāyas are compared to a reflection of the moon in water. The Buddha is the dharmakāya and he manifests in the two form kāyas to help other beings with no thought of doing so. In the same way, the moon reflecting in the water doesn't think, "I must shine on the water" and the reflection doesn't think, "I am here because the moon is shining." It is just the presence of the moon in the sky and the presence of water on the ground that make a reflection possible. In the same way, the two form kāyas are not the result of the dharmakāya thinking, "I must manifest in the form kāyas" or the form kāyas thinking, "I am created by the dharmakāya."

### *The Ten Powers*

[245] The first power of the Buddhas is perfect knowledge of the appropriate and inappropriate. When bodhiṣattvas make the commitment to reach enlightenment for the sake of all beings, they don't abandon this commitment. Ordinary beings, however, make promises and after a time may break them and perhaps later keep them again. But the power behind the knowledge of appropriateness becomes a very firm commitment that is never abandoned and allows the Buddhas to know the cause of any given situation or any action. The Buddhas know what should bring a particular effect and what is due to a certain cause. For instance, they know that every virtuous action will have a pleasant result and every nonvirtuous action will eventually result in a painful outcome.

The second power of the Buddhas is knowing the fruition of actions which means fully understanding the workings of karma. This power comes from having paid great attention to the law of karma while practicing on the path and in trying to help others understand karma. For example, an arhat wouldn't know the cause of the blue and yellow color on a peacock's feather, but the Buddha would know exactly what action gave rise to that particular effect.

The third power is knowing the degree of intelligence of persons. On the path bodhisattvas taught persons according to their level of understanding. They could see that some had very great diligence, others not; some were very intelligent, others not. Accordingly, bodhisattvas gave teachings that were suitable for the pupils at the appropriate level.

The fourth power is knowing the various temperaments of beings. The bodhisattvas on the path saw the different dispositions and temperaments of beings. They saw that some were influenced mostly by anger, so they taught them the remedy for anger. Others had a major problem with desire, so they taught the remedy for desire. Still others were mostly obscured by ignorance. Some had too many thoughts and received yet another remedy. When bodhisattvas reached Buddhahood, they then had the full knowledge of the temperaments of beings.

The fifth power is the knowledge of the interests of beings. The bodhisattvas knew that some persons were attracted to the hīnayāna and others were more interested in the mahāyāna. They knew that some were attracted to the practice of generosity, while others preferred to practice discipline, and still others preferred meditation. Since they knew exactly what each being preferred practicing, they knew exactly the wishes and interests of all beings when they became Buddhas.

The sixth power is the knowledge of the path which leads everywhere. On the path as a bodhisattva they became familiar with all levels of practice of all the yānas. As a result they could see that the various paths lead to the different states of saṃsāra and nirvāṇa and see the path that leads to less suffering, the path that leads to immediate happiness and the path of eternal happiness. This familiarity with all yānas on the path results in the Buddha's knowledge of the path that goes everywhere.

[246] The seventh power is knowing meditative stability without any defilement. The Buddhas know what is true and false meditation because while they were practicing the path they emphasized meditation in their practice and

learned the correct way of meditating. They also learned the mistakes that could arise and how to eliminate these mistakes.

The eighth power is remembering former states. The Buddhas can remember clearly all their former states in saṃsāra—not just one or two lifetimes, but all the lifetimes since the beginning of saṃsāra. This is a power that comes from their practice on the path. They took every opportunity to practice virtue no matter how small and as a result it gave them the power of remembering former states.

The ninth power is divine vision which means that the Buddhas can see what is going to happen to beings in the future. They can see which birth a person is going to take, what kind of state they're going to. This power is the result of having looked after all beings with great compassion while practicing the path.

The tenth power is the knowledge of the purification of all impurities so the Buddhas know that impurities of any kind have been totally eliminated. If somebody were to have this feeling before reaching Buddhahood, it would be only an illusion because it is impossible for anyone except a Buddha to have eliminated all impurities and to know this with certainty. The arhats have only partial freedom from impurities. This power of knowing that all impurities have been pacified was gained on the path by having taught others the way to exhaust all impurities. For themselves it was gained by practicing meditation.

[247] These ten qualities are called powers because they're extremely powerful and they're compared to three analogies. They're compared to a vajra which can pierce armor, destroy walls, and fell the trees of ignorance. So ignorance representing three kinds of obscurations is compared to armor, a solid wall, and to a very thick forest.

### *The Four Fearlessnesses*

[248] There are four fearlessnesses. First, the Buddhas are fearless because they can say that they have reached perfect purification with nothing more to purify. They can say they have perfect knowledge without any fear of contradiction because they know everything without exception. The cause of this fearlessness is that they were always ready to give teaching to whoever wanted them with the same loving consideration for all beings.

The second fearlessness is related to teaching other beings. The Buddhas have no fear that they may be contradicted by anyone. No one could ever prove the Buddhas to be wrong when they show the obstacles on the path.

The third fearlessness is that the Buddhas put into practice the removal of impurities through the five levels of practice and the complete 37 factors of enlightenment. The Buddhas are perfectly sure that the path can lead to enlightenment. They are not worried that anyone might contradict him because they know that the path being taught is the path that is complete and can provide complete enlightenment.

The second and third fearlessnesses are for the benefit of other beings. They are acquired on the path before the Buddhas actually became enlightened. On the path the bodhisattvas strive to act virtuously in all ways possible and to eliminate even very small impurities continuously. As a result they develop the two kinds of fearlessnesses of how to relinquish obscurations and to guide themselves on the correct path to enlightenment.

The fourth fearlessness is in respect to self. The Buddhas can state that they have overcome all impurities without being worried of anyone contradicting them because during the practice of the path they never had any pride when they were teaching other beings.

[249] What is the purpose or function of the four fearlessnesses? Since the Buddhas know everything, the function of the fearlessnesses is to raise everyone to this level of knowledge. The second function is to help other beings do the same. Thirdly, the Buddhas have achieved their goal of unsurpassable and perfect enlightenment and helped others to do likewise. Finally, they tell others truthfully the meaning of what they themselves have realized because great sages are not hindered when they give their teachings.

[250] There are examples for the different fearlessnesses. A lion in the forest is never afraid because he knows he is the strongest animal and is therefore is never worried about meeting other wild animals. In the same way, wherever or among whatever beings the Buddha finds himself, he will always remain fearless. His skills will always remain the same because at no point will he ever have any doubts about his ability to teach because he knows what he says is true. He will also never be disturbed by feelings of hope or fear about having disciples.

### *The 18 Distinctive Qualities*

[251] The 18 qualities are divided into three groups—those qualities related to behavior, those related to understanding, and those related to activity. The first six qualities are concerned with the Buddha's physical behavior. Whenever the Buddhas do something, it is impossible for it to be adulterated by a mistake. Most of

the time the arhats will act very correctly, but sometimes they make a mistake. So this is why correctness is a distinct quality of the Buddhas not shared by anyone else. The second quality is related to the speech of the Buddhas who do not speak in a meaningless or useless way. The third quality is related to the mind of the Buddhas whose mindfulness never decreases. Ordinary beings and even arhats will forget from time to time but it is totally impossible for the Buddhas to ever forget anything. The fourth quality is related to the Buddha's mind which rests in meditation all the time. The fifth quality is that the Buddhas never thought of deceiving others. The whole time they're in a loving disposition, a very truthful disposition, without being encumbered by uncompassionate thoughts. The sixth quality of Buddhas is that they never act casually without first examining very carefully how to act so they are never frivolous in their actions.

[252] The next six qualities are qualities of understanding. The seventh quality is that Buddhas do not suffer any diminution of their aspiration to benefit beings. The eighth is that there is never any decrease of their diligence. Ninth, there is never any decrease of their memory. Tenth, there is never any degradation of their understanding. Eleventh, there is never any change in their perfect liberation. Twelfth, they never lose their perception of perfect jñāna.

[253] The third group of qualities are the qualities of actions. These deeds are again subdivided into three distinctive qualities of activity and the three distinctive qualities of jñāna. Buddha activity means that whenever Buddhas act, their physical actions are preceded and followed by jñāna. Likewise, their speech and their

thoughts are also preceded and followed by jñāna. None of the actions of the Buddhas are done without great care or without a very precise examination of the situation. Before they act, they see the outcome with their jñāna and act accordingly. After the action has been accomplished, the Buddhas will accompany it with their jñāna to make sure that it was properly completed.

The three qualities of jñāna of the Buddhas are completely unhindered by past, present, and future. This means there are no emotional or cognitive obscurations to hinder their practice. It is completely free and fluid and can know everything without hindrance.

### *The Function of 18 Qualities*

[254] For the great sages there are six qualities of behavior—making no mistakes, no chatter, no forgetfulness, no mental agitation, no random thoughts, and no casual action. There are the six qualities of realization—no decrease of aspiration, diligence, memory, perfectly pure prajñā, perfect liberation, and having the jñāna of liberation which sees all aspects of the knowable. Three qualities pertain to the Buddha's activity and three pertain to jñāna.
[255] The Buddhas have realization of these 18 qualities which makes it possible for them to turn the wheel of dharma, have great compassion, and overcome all defilements. Because of this they can perfectly and fearlessly turn the wheel of dharma.
[256] These 18 qualities are compared to space. The elements of earth, water, fire, and air have their own characteristics. Earth is solid, water fluid, air moving, and fire hot and burning. These qualities of the elements are

unlike those of space because space allows things to take place in it. In the same way, the 18 distinctive qualities are only possessed by the Buddha. Ordinary beings do not have the special distinctive qualities of a Buddha anymore than the Buddhas have the faults of ordinary beings.

### *The 32 Qualities of Maturity*

The qualities of maturity are expressed by the 32 marks of the Buddha. They're called the beautiful marks or marks of excellence because they are special attributes of Buddhahood. They are also called the qualities of maturity because they are the result of the long process of gathering virtue along the path.

[257] The first mark is that the Buddha's feet are perfectly level and bear the mark of a thousand spoked wheel (Skt. *dharmacakra*). This signifies that while the Buddha was on the path he had taken and observed the vows properly, had respected his teachers, and had gathered a great deal of virtue. The second mark is that his feet are very wide and their ankles are not visible. This indicates that he had practiced all the aspects of virtue to a very high degree. The third mark is his fingers and toes are long and this signifies that the Buddha while on the path protected beings who were about to be killed and saved them from death. The fourth mark is the digits of his hands and feet are connected by a web signifying that whenever the Buddha was with people who were disagreeing, he tried to bring them together.

[258] The fifth mark is his skin is very soft and smooth like a youth which is the sign that while on the path the Buddha gave many clothes and food away to other people.

The sixth mark is that his body has seven elevated parts corresponding to the two tops of the feet, the tops of the hands, the shoulders, and the back of the neck. So there are seven parts that are nicely rounded and elevated which came from having given food and drink to other beings while practicing the path. The seventh mark is his calves are like those of an antelope meaning that they are very strong, solid, and muscular signifying that during the path he learned all the aspects of the five branches of Buddhist knowledge. The eighth sign is that his private parts are sunk into recesses as an elephant's signifying that the Buddha always kept a person's secrets and did not tell them to others.

[259] The ninth mark is that his torso is like a lion's meaning it is very majestic and wide. This signifies that the Buddha had looked after others with great care and concern and practiced virtue himself with great perseverance. The tenth mark is that his clavicle is not hollow, but filled in with flesh with no spaces in between the two bones. This signifies that on the path the Buddha was very generous particularly to the sick by giving them medicine. The 11th mark is the tops of his shoulders are nicely rounded signifying that on the path the Buddha used proper speech by speaking only appropriately and kindly and protected others from fear. The 12th mark is his arms are soft, round, and very smooth and even. This signifies that on the path the Buddha was always a friend for others helping them as diligently as possible.

[260] The 13th mark is that his arms are very long, reaching the level of his knees, showing that on the path whenever someone came to ask for something, the person's expectations were always completely fulfilled. The 14th

mark is that the Buddha's body is perfectly pure and surrounded by a bright aura showing that on the path the Buddha made relentless efforts to practice the ten virtues. The 15th mark is that there are three lines on his neck which make a picture of a conch shell signifying the special ability of the Buddha to teach the 84,000 aspects of the dharma. This also represents the fact that on the path the Buddha always served the sick and nursed them and gave them medicine. The 16th mark is that the cheeks of the Buddha are like those of a king of beasts (lion) showing that the Buddha didn't chatter uselessly and always endeavored to lead other beings to practice what was good and wholesome.

[261] The 17th mark is the Buddha has 40 teeth with 20 in the upper and 20 on the lower jaw. This shows that on the path the Buddha had the same attitude towards all beings treating all with equal kindness because all beings were once our parents. This sameness of attitude is symbolized by the same number of teeth and is because the Buddha never said any harsh words to anyone. The 18th mark of the Buddha is that his teeth are perfectly clean and beautifully aligned signifying that the Buddhas always brought others into harmony and what Buddhas said was always the truth. The 19th mark is the Buddha's teeth are completely immaculate and even so not one of his teeth is longer than others. This signifies that while on the path, the Buddha gave away his possessions and made his living honestly without any deceit. The 20th mark is that the canine teeth of the Buddha are perfectly and completely white showing that on the path all their physical, verbal, and mental actions were perfectly honest and straightforward.

[262] The 21st mark is that the Buddha's tongue is long and endless and inconceivable indicating that the Buddha has the ability to speak the dharma which is of a very profound meaning. This particular mark is the sign that on the path the Buddha spoke softly and never said anything coarse. The 22nd mark is that the Buddha had a perfect faculty of taste meaning that whenever he comes into contact with food it produces the most exquisite taste. This is because the Buddha always gave those who were in need remedies that were agreeable and good for them. The 23rd mark is the Buddha has a voice as sweet as the kalavinka bird which has a beautiful song. During the path the Buddha always spoke in a very soft, smooth voice that always said what is true and relevant and pleasant to beings who heard it.

[263] The 24th mark is the Buddha's eyes are pale and delicate like blue lotuses. This shows that while on the path the Buddha treated people as though they were his only sons just as a mother has the greatest love for her only son. The 25th mark of the Buddha is that his eyelashes are as handsome as those of an ox meaning they are very long and nicely separated. This signifies the Buddha's absence of anger in the practice of the path and that he never behaved hypocritically. The 26th mark is the Buddha's face is very clear, white, and beautiful. During the path the Buddha always showed the greatest respect for special beings like other bodhisattvas and always praised them with great reverence. Also he has an immaculate white *ūrṇa* hair which is a very fine hair between his eyebrows. The 27th mark is that Buddha has a mound on his head and one cannot see the end of that mound meaning that on the path, the Buddha had great reverence for his guru and other

teachers and bodhisattvas. Literally, it says that he carries other bodhisattvas on his head which is a sign of greatest respect. The 28th mark is that the skin of the Buddha is pure and fine. This indicates that on the path he always strove to do good because his mind was very manageable. The 29th mark is his skin is the color of gold which is the sign of having served the Buddhas and made offerings to them in all possible ways during the practice of the path.

[264] The 30th mark of the Buddha is that the hairs of his body are very soft and fine with one coming out of each pore and curling to the right and towards the top of the body. This signifies the great manageability of his mind and his great efforts in the practice of virtue during the path. The 31st mark is that the Buddha's hair is impeccable and has a slightly bluish tinge like a deep blue jewel. This signifies the Buddha was always very kind and loving towards everyone. The 32nd mark is the Buddha's body is perfectly proportioned and is compared to the roundness of a banyan tree. This shows that the Buddha went to different places where he practiced meditation and led other beings onto the path of meditation.

[265] Finally, it is said that the Buddha has a firm body and the strength of Nārāyaṇa[8] which is a general quality of his whole body and not a mark. This signifies the great respect that the Buddha always showed to other Buddhas and bodhisattvas on the path and the praises that he offered them. These 32 marks and the 64 qualities are explained in this same order in the *Jewel Sūtra* (*Ratnadarikasūtra*).

8 Nārāyaṇa refers to the Indian god Vishnu.

### *Examples of the Qualities*

[266] The form of the Buddhas is compared to the autumn moon in a cloudless sky. This example has been used before in connection with the form kāyas. Here the pure disciples of the bodhisattvas are compared to a lake of pure water. The reflection of the moon in pure water is very clear showing all the qualities of the moon. In this way, the bodhisattvas can see the Buddhas directly in their maṇḍala so that they see the sambhogakāya body with all the marks and signs of perfection. However, ordinary beings and śrāvakas do not see this sambhogakāya.

[267] There are four sets of qualities of the Buddha. First are the ten powers of the Buddha which are called this because they can defeat and destroy all obscurations and cannot be harmed by this negativity. These powers are compared to a vajra because a vajra is made of a substance that has the power to destroy anything else and cannot be harmed by anything.

[268] The next set of qualities are the four fearlessnesses. Fearlessness means the Buddha never has the feeling that he cannot understand something or becomes discouraged. This is compared to a lion because a lion is unafraid of other animals. In the same way, the Buddhas never have any doubt or think, "Will I know this?" or "Maybe I will make a mistake."

The third set is the 18 distinctive attributes of the Buddha which are compared to space. These qualities belong to the Buddha and no one else because space has few qualities in common with the other elements.

The fourth set of qualities represents the two form kāyas and the 32 marks of the Buddha and these are compared to the reflection of the moon in water. When the moon is in the sky, it doesn't think "I will reflect in the water." In the same way, buddha activity occurs when the time is ripe and manifests spontaneously without any conscious thought.

[269] The ten powers are divided into three groups with the first six powers representing a vajra vanquishing cognitive obscurations. These are the knowledge of appropriateness, full fruition of actions, degree of intelligence, different temperaments, different wishes, and the path that leads everywhere. The next three powers destroy meditative obscurations. These are the power of meditative stability, remembering former states, and divine vision. These three are like a vajra because they destroy the hindrances to meditative balance. Finally, the last power destroys the fine subconscious traces left behind. This last power is the one whereby the Buddha knows that all defilements have been totally pacified.

[270] The obscurations are also represented by an example. The cognitive obscuration is compared to thick armor which is pierced by the vajra of the Buddha's first six powers. The meditative obscurations are compared to a thick wall which is destroyed by the next three powers of the Buddha. The subconscious traces are compaied to a tree which is felled by the last power of the Buddha. It is said that the powers of the great sage, the Buddha, are like a vajra because they are firm, resistant, steadfast, and unshakeable. They are firm because they have the quality of changelessness because once these powers manifest they are like the strong essence of phenomena. They are steadfast in that they are not subject to change. They are unshakeable like a vajra.

[272] The second set of qualities of the Buddha is related to fearlessness. The Buddha is compared to a lion because a lion is fearless, unconcerned, stable, and has supreme skill. A lion is fearless in the midst of other animals and the Buddha is fearless in the midst of a gathering of people. When the Buddha is teaching, he is never afraid that his teaching won't show the way or point to the genuine path because he knows it is the complete path that leads to Buddhahood. A lion is fearless in the midst of other animals because it is stronger than any of them. Likewise, the Buddha is fearless because he knows all phenomena directly. The lion is self-reliant because it doesn't need anything to protect him. In the same way, the Buddha is independent because he doesn't need to fear that anyone might defeat him. Thirdly, a lion has stability in his powers because the strength of a lion is always there. In the same way, the pure mind of the Buddha is perfectly clear and stable at all times and cognizant of all phenomena. The Buddha is never impure so his qualities are always stable.

[274] The fourth feature that the Buddha and the lion have in common is supreme skill. The lion has physical skill that never diminishes; so he never needs to fear. In the same way, the Buddha has completely transcended all ignorance. So he has no fear of losing his power.

[275] The 18 distinctive qualities of the Buddha are compared to space. The five stages of enlightenment can be compared to the five elements. One may divide beings into five different kinds. First are ordinary beings who are completely under the power of illusion and delusion. With more understanding are the śrāvakas who understand the nonexistence of a personal self so their minds are already clearer. Further along are the pratyekabuddhas whose

understanding goes further than that of the śrāvakas in that they also understand the nonexistence of outer objects, but don't understand the nonexistence of the perceiving mind. Still further along are the bodhisattvas who have the understanding of both the personal and phenomenal self, but they haven't completely mastered it. Finally, comes the Buddha who has full, complete understanding of both aspects of existence.

The mind of ordinary beings is compared to the earth element which is very dense. The water element is less dense or lighter than earth and corresponds to the śrāvakas. The element of fire is even less dense and corresponds to the pratyekabuddhas. The air element is still less dense and corresponds to the bodhisattvas. Finally, the element of space is compared to the 18 distinctive qualities of the Buddha. The Buddha is further compared to all the elements combined. The earth gives the world its solidity, water its fluidity, fire its warmth, and air its movement. So the Buddhas provide the basis for all qualities. They are like space in that they're beyond all characteristics of the world and beyond the world. This means they are beyond any comparison with ordinary beings, bodhisattvas, etc.

[277] These 32 qualities appear different but are actually indivisible from one another and just represent different facets of the same thing. This inseparability is compared to a jewel—one cannot actually separate the color or the brilliance or the shapes seen in a jewel from each other because they are completely inseparable from the actual jewel. In the same way, these 32 qualities of the Buddha are inseparable from the dharmakāya.

[278] The 32 qualities of maturity bring contentment, happiness, and joy. These 32 marks are expressed in the

two form kāyas: the nirmāṇakāya and the sambhogakāya which represent the perfect expression of the mahāyāna dharma. Those far from purity are ordinary beings. The śrāvakas see the form kāyas as the nirmāṇakāya. Those who are close to purity, the bodhisattvas, see the form kāyas as the sambhogakāya. The pure ones are compared in the example to those who see the moon directly in the sky and those who are impure to those who see the moon reflected in the water.

# CHAPTER 10

## *Buddha Activity*

[280] This chapter is divided into spontaneous buddha activity which happen naturally without any effort and unceasing buddha activity which never stops.

The Buddhas always act spontaneously. The Buddhas know the various temperaments of beings, the various dispositions of beings, their dominant tendencies, and their aspirations. Seeing their temperaments allows them to know what means to use to educate them. Some people are helped best by showing them an example of a certain type of behavior. For example, if they see the peaceful and very controlled behavior of a Buddha, they will have a great feeling of faith and this will lead them to the dharma. But others respond to miracles, so the Buddhas will show them miracles. Some just respond to teachings so the Buddhas will just give teachings to them. The Buddhas also know that some beings are ready to work on higher levels and others are ready for total liberation, so they place them on the path that corresponds to their level of ability and aspiration.

The Buddhas know precisely the time and the place their activity is needed without any thought and they act effortlessly at the correct moment in a way which is perfectly appropriate to the needs of beings.

[281] Buddha activity is unceasing. The qualities of the

Buddhas are a sum of all the good qualities of meditation and the various paths of the Buddhas are like an ocean containing many jewels. The Buddhas are also compared to the sun. They have completed the two accumulations of virtue and insight and these are compared to the sun because vegetables, grass, trees, and everything needs sunlight to grow. In the same way, with the perfect sunlight of the Buddhas' accumulations all beings can be brought to spiritual maturity. Finally, the Buddhas are compared to space because the Buddhas are without beginning, middle, or end; they are deep and vast because they have achieved all the yānas.

These three examples show what makes them Buddhas. They can see the seed of Buddhahood in the mind of all beings and they can see that it makes no difference whether beings are presently in a higher or a lower state of existence. They also see there is no difference between someone who is practicing the path or not; the seed is within all beings without any distinction. This treasure is presently hidden by impurities, but they know how to extract it from its covering. The clouds of obscurations can be removed by the Buddhas' compassion which is similar to a wind blowing away all the clouds from the sun. In more detail:

[282] Buddha activity is spontaneous because through their knowledge of variety, they do not need to think, "For whom am I doing this?" or "What way should I so this?" because they automatically know for whom and by what means they are going to act. Through the knowledge of how-it-is they understand that everything is nonexistent, unborn, and has no actual reality. So when they are acting, they do not hesitate wondering if everything is real.

Knowing true emptiness, they know precisely how to act. In this way buddha activity is spontaneous and devoid of any thought and at the same time corresponds exactly to the needs of the beings they are helping.

[285] There are six points which describe the unceasing activity of the Buddha: release or the definite freedom from saṃsāra; attaining freedom through the two accumulations; the fruition of this freedom which is the achievement of Buddhahood; that all beings can achieve this fruition; the achievement of this fruition; that all beings have buddha nature, but they cannot see it because it is veiled by the obscurations; and finally the removal of these obscurations. In more detail:

[286] The first point is that through buddha activity the Buddhas help all beings enter the path helping release them from saṃsāra. Through buddha activity a being will reach the first bodhisattva level, then the second, and so on until he goes beyond saṃsāra. Secondly, freedom is attained by entering the bodhisattva path and practicing the two accumulations of virtue and insight. Thirdly, the fruition of beings established in the various bodhisattva levels is the state of a Buddha. Fourthly, when beings try to progress through the various bodhisattva levels, they encounter cognitive and emotional obscurations and the subconscious imprints left by karma. Fifthly, all obscurations have been removed when enlightenment is achieved. And sixthly, the great compassion of the Buddhas provides all the necessary conditions for destroying these obscurations.

[287] These six points are illustrated by six similes. The three freedoms achieved with the mastery of the ten bodhisattva levels are illustrated by an example of the ocean. The practice of the two accumulations are represented by

an example of the sun. The achievement of Buddhahood is represented by space and all beings who can achieve this are compared to a treasure. And the various obscurations are symbolized by clouds.

[288] The reasons for using these similes are as follows. The ten levels of the bodhisattva path are symbolized by an ocean because when beings enter the successive levels of the bodhisattva path, they are endowed with a great number of qualities which are like precious jewels. The state of a bodhisattva on the tenth level is compared to a great ocean because the ocean contains many fabulous jewels which are compared to the qualities of meditation, the powers of perfect memory, intuitive cognition, and the like which a bodhisattva at this level possesses.

The two accumulations are symbolized by the sun because if there were no sun, there would be no warmth and nothing would grow; so the conditions for life would be absent. In the same way, the two accumulations are like the sun in that they are the two vital factors needed to attain liberation.

Thirdly, enlightenment is compared to space because it has no beginning, center, or end so one cannot say that space is this or that because space has no solid existence. Buddhahood is similar in that it is very vast, very profound, and cannot be described in any way.

The possession of buddha nature is compared to a buried treasure because a treasure can provide all one's material needs. But if it is covered with earth, it has only the potential to do so. However, if one uses effort to take the treasure from the ground, one can have everything one wishes for. In the same way, buddha nature is within all beings but it is covered with defilements. But if one removes all the defilements with the effort of gathering the two accumulations, one can ultimately achieve Buddhahood.

[290] In the fifth example, the obscurations are compared to clouds. Clouds appear in the sky and will sometimes veil the sun, but they are not an intrinsic part of the sky or the sun. They are only fleeting phenomena which can be removed. When the clouds are covering the sun, one cannot feel the sunshine; when the clouds are removed, the sun is perceived in its original purity. In the same way, there are fleeting impurities veiling our buddha nature, but these can be removed because they are not an inherent part of our buddha essence.

The sixth comparison is between the great compassion of the Buddhas and a great wind. As long as clouds cover the sun, it cannot shine. As long as impurities are present, beings cannot achieve liberation. They need the Buddha's compassion to remove the impurities that are veiling their true nature; this compassion acts like a strong wind removing all the impurities of beings.

[291] Buddha activity has an unceasing character because from the very beginning, the Buddhas committed themselves to the goal of achieving Buddhahood for the sake of other beings. Secondly, the Buddhas saw the similarity between themselves and other beings and understood that if they managed to achieve Buddhahood, then everyone else could also become a Buddha. A third reason for this ceaselessness is that the number of beings is infinite and the Buddhas will never stop acting to help them until saṃsāra is finished. So as long as there are beings in saṃsāra, buddha activity will continue.

[292] There are nine examples to explain how the

spontaneous and ceaseless quality of buddha activity applies to beings. The first example of the spontaneous quality is a fictional example of the god Indra who is the chief god of the 33 gods in Indian mythology. The second example is of the drum of the gods which illustrates how the Buddha's speech can manifest everywhere without any effort on the part of the Buddha. The drum of the gods is in the heaven of the 33 gods and is a true example of this place. There is, of course, some fantasy in the way the example is presented. The third example is of clouds which do not need any conscious effort to create rain and illustrates how the mind of the Buddha works. The fourth example using the god Brahma illustrates all the emanations of the Buddha. The fifth example compares the Buddha's jñānas to sunshine because the sun radiates everywhere and in the same way the Buddha's jñāna knows everything perfectly clearly. Finally, the last three examples illustrate the mystery, the inconceivability of the Buddha's mind, speech, and body which work effortlessly to help beings. The Buddha's mind is illustrated by a wish-fulfilling gem. The seventh example of the Buddha's speech is an echo illustrating the inconceivability of the dharma which can be heard everywhere by those who are ready, but doesn't need any conscious thought by the Buddha to produce it. The eighth example illustrates the inconceivability of the physical manifestation of the Buddha and uses the example of space which occurs everywhere, at any time, and in any form as required by the needs of beings. In more detail:

[293] The physical emanation of the Buddha is compared to an imaginary example of Indra. Imagine the ground of the whole world becoming lapis lazuli that is so clear that

it is like a mirror which reflects the heaven above where the god Brahma is surround by a multitude of beautiful goddesses. Staying in his palace called the "perfectly victorious" he is enjoying many worldly delights. The lapis lazuli is so clear that everything happening in heaven can be seen reflected on the ground. The effect is that individuals feel that they would make prayers and gather the virtue necessary so they could enjoy such delights. This happens without any action or intention of Indra, it is just the reflection which produces virtuous activity.

[299] In the same way, bodhisattvas who are full of faith, diligence, intelligence, and are engaged in the practice of virtue can see the sambhogakāya directly in contrast to ordinary beings who don't have the possibility of meeting the supreme nirmāṇakāya, but know the Buddha's teaching by his footprints left after he has gone. So bodhisattvas who have faith and all these good qualities can see the Buddha with his 32 marks and all the beautiful signs. They will see the Buddhas walking, standing, sitting, sleeping, and proclaiming the teachings of peace. Sometimes they will see him in meditation without speaking and sometimes they will see miracles. So beings with the right virtue will see the Buddha without the Buddha thinking, "I must do this." This vision of the Buddha will inspire them to achieve Buddhahood and they will be enthusiastic in their devotion and apply themselves in their conduct to become a Buddha.

All the Buddha's manifestations are completely without thought on his part; however, the beings of the world can see and hear the Buddha turning the wheel of dharma bringing an infinite number of beings on the path to enlightenment. When ordinary beings see the form of the

Buddha and hear his words, they do not realize that these are appearances in their mind. Even though they don't understand this, it is very important because those less developed have the seed of liberation in their mind. Then gradually depending on their experiences, they will enter the mahāyāna path and eventually see the inner Buddha, that is the dharmakāya, with the eyes of jñāna.

[306] Expanding this example, if all the frightening places such as cliffs and abysses were eliminated and covered with lapis lazuli which was completely free from impurities making it a very fine mirror, one could see the various paradises. But later on, little by little, the ground would gradually lose its polish and little by little the reflection of paradise would begin to disappear. But having seen the reflection, beings would be inspired and many men and women would continue to practice and make offerings to enter into paradise.

[308] In the same way, when the Buddha appears in the pure lapis lazuli surface of the mind, individuals are inspired to reach the same level as the Buddha. Accordingly, these songs of the victorious ones (the bodhisattvas) will cultivate the bodhicitta so there will be a strong wish and great joy to try to nurture all the qualities of understanding so that they can achieve enlightenment.

[309] These reflections can change because when the ground is very pure, the lapis lazuli is like a mirror; but when the ground is less pure, the reflection disappears. In the same way, when beings have great faith and devotion and many pure qualities, they can see the Buddha; but when their mind are less pure, they cannot see the Buddha anymore. So Indra and the Buddhas are always present and their appearance depends on the purity of the beings.

[310] In the second example, the drum of the gods is only a term for the spontaneous manifestation of the sound of dharma. Because of the previous virtue of the gods, the sound of dharma can be heard spontaneously in some heavens. One can hear the constant sound of the words "impermanence," "suffering," "no-self," and "peace" without anyone being there to make the sounds.

[312] This example illustrates how the speech of the Buddha can manifest without any effort or thought on his part. The Buddha's teaching can be heard anywhere by spiritually developed individuals. Buddha's speech, however, is far beyond the drum of the gods because the sound of the drum can't be heard by nongods while the Buddha's speech can.

[321] The third example compares the mind of the Buddha with clouds. In a country with a monsoon, the clouds are constantly producing huge quantities of rain during the summer which, of course, allows the crops to grow. In the same way, the mind and compassion of the Buddha constantly produces the rain of dharma so that the crops of virtue of beings can flourish. This rain is the rain of the four noble truths: (1) If one is sick then, (2) one must find the cause of the sickness to be cured. Next, (3) one must be willing to undergo treatment for the illness and (4) one must then take the medicine. In terms of the four truths: (1) one must understand that there is suffering, (2) one must find the cause of this suffering which is karma and the defilements. Next, (3) when one has eliminated the causes of the suffering, the suffering will stop. Finally, (4) the truth of the path is like a medicine which liberates one from suffering. So this is what is meant by saying that the Buddha pours the rains of the four truths on beings.

[334] How the Buddha emanates is illustrated by a fictitious fourth example of Brahma. Of the three dimensions of saṃsāra: the desire, the form, and the formless realm, Brahma resides in his own heaven in the form realm. He remains there continuously and has no thought of manifesting anywhere else. However, his emanation can be seen in all the other godly heavens without any deliberate intention on the part of Brahma. In the same way, the Buddha appears in the sambhogakāya form to individuals who are spiritually mature and to the less spiritually mature in the nirmāṇakāya form while the Buddha himself resides in the dharmakāya.

[336] Having had five visions, our present Buddha, the Śākyamuni Buddha, left Tuṣita heaven to enter our world. His mother had a dream of a six tusked elephant and he took birth in the garden at Lumbini. He then spent many years at the palace of his father learning many different skills and enjoying the company of friends and consorts. Disillusioned with saṃsāra, he left the palace and for the next six years practiced great austerities. Then he tackled all the negative forces and defeated them and achieved Buddhahood under the bodhi tree. Having reached enlightenment, he went to Vārāṇasī and in the deer park there turned the first wheel of the dharma. So while the Buddha was available to those who were spiritually ready at the time, the Buddha could be seen in the dharmakāya illustrating that the Buddha can manifest in many ways and never leave the dharmakāya.

[337] The fifth example illustrates how the jñāna of the Buddha functions using the example of the sun. The sun without thinking can shine simultaneously everywhere on the earth. Different flowers react differently to sunlight;

lotuses open and kumuta flowers close automatically. In the same way, the Buddhas radiate the light of dharma on the lotus flowers on the mind of beings and some will open up and feel devotion and practice the teachings while others will react like the kumuta flowers and close up and continue to wander in saṃsāra. When this happens it is not the fault of the Buddhas just as the sun cannot be blamed for the kumuta flowers closing.

When the Buddhas are turning the wheel of dharma, they do not have any particular thought or objective in mind, for instance, they don't think, "I must establish the dharma first in India so it will flourish in this place" and so on. Instead they teach the dharma whenever it is needed and to whomever can benefit from it. Through the natural power of buddha activity, the teachings take place and beings receive them and work with them to reach liberation.

[340] The example of the sun is limited because the activity of the Buddha's jñāna goes much further than the sun. The sun can remove only ordinary darkness while the Buddha's jñāna can dispel the darkness of ignorance and give exact knowledge of the true nature of all phenomena.

[346] The sixth example illustrates the mystery of the Buddha's mind. It is a mystery because it is so inconceivable and subtle. It is compared to a wish-fulfilling gem. When there was a wish-fulfilling gem, persons received whatever they wished for. Even though they may have wanted many different things, their wishes were fulfilled with no thought or intention of the gem. In the same way, there are many beings who have different aspirations, wishes, and interests and the Buddhas give them whatever teaching is relevant to their needs—if it

leads to a higher existence. Some beings need the hīnayāna teachings, some the mahāyāna teachings, and some the vajrayāna teachings and all these teachings come without any conscious thought of the Buddhas.

[350] The seventh example compares the mystery of the activity of the Buddha's speech, which is inconceivable and subtle, like an echo. The sound of an echo is due to the cognitive faculties of others, while the echo itself is devoid of any thought or intention. An echo does not come from the inside or the outside. In the same way, the Buddha's speech manifests according to an individual's spiritual maturity, while the sound of dharma itself is devoid of any thought or effort. It abides neither inside nor outside the Buddha's body.

[352] The eighth example compares the mystery of the Buddha's form to space which is inconceivable and subtle. Space doesn't have any substance, yet it provides the background for everything to happen. In the same way, the body of the Buddha does not have any real existence, but it is there to help beings everywhere. Also the Buddha doesn't think, "I am going to be in this form and in this particular place," but whenever beings are ready, a form of the Buddha will manifest to help them.

[354] The ninth example compares the great compassion of the Buddha to the earth. The earth without any thought provides the basis for everything to grow and once it has grown it allows everything to continue to live. So the earth is the basis of life without any thought. In the same way, the Buddhas have the full and direct knowledge of the nature of everything and spontaneously the qualities of body, speech, and mind provide a ground for all the virtues and good qualities to develop and allow these qualities to flourish on the earth.

### *The Purpose of these Examples*

[356] In ordinary life, when we want to achieve something, we have to put effort into it. So when we hear about buddha activity we might have doubts because it is hard to conceive of effortless activity. These nine examples are given to remove these doubts about how the Buddha's activity is completely effortless.

[357] These nine examples were taught in detail in the Ornament of the Light of Jñāna sūtra and there are two reasons for studying them: to remove any doubts about effortless activity of the Buddha and, on a deeper level, to bring the bodhisattva quickly to Buddhahood.

[360] These nine examples illustrate the manifestation of the body, speech, and all-pervasiveness of the Buddha's mind, the emanations of the Buddha, the all-embracing qualities of his jñāna, the mysterious aspect of his body, speech, and mind, and his compassion.

[363] In ordinary existence we know only of activity which is connected with physical or mental effort. This contrasts with the Buddha whose activity is effortless because he is free from any thought to accomplish his activity. This absence of thought is because the Buddha possesses the jñāna of how-it-is which allows him to understand that all phenomena are void. He doesn't not need to think, "Now I will act in this way." And with the jñāna of variety, the Buddha can act completely effortlessly and spontaneously.

[365] In the examples, the physical manifestation of the Buddha is represented by a lapis lazuli ground, the Buddha's speech by the drum of the gods, and the Buddha's mind by the clouds and so on.

[372] Someone may think, "Well, one example would have been sufficient, why present all nine examples?" The reason is that buddha activity is so subtle that it cannot be represented by just one example. Examples have limitations and the limitations of each example call for another example. In the first example of the lapis lazuli ground, the limitation of the example is that Indra's reflection is only a physical reflection; but when the Buddha appears this reflection is also accompanied by the sound of dharma giving rise to another example of the sound of dharma. The second example of the drum of the gods illustrates the effortless manifestation of the Buddha's speech, but it doesn't go far enough because the drum is sometimes beneficial and sometimes not depending on whether people take heed to what is heard. All the words of the Buddha's speech, however, help beings to reach spiritual maturity all the time.

[373] The third example of a rain cloud doesn't go far enough because a rain cloud can bring short-term benefit to beings, but it cannot eliminate impurities. Buddha activity has the additional long-term benefit of reducing the negativity of beings so a fourth example of Brahma is needed. Brahma can have a very positive influence on those who are directly around him, but he cannot be compared to the Buddha because he cannot remove the seed of the negativity.

[374] In the fifth example the sun dispels darkness but the sun can only dispel darkness during the day and at night the darkness returns, while Buddha activity can permanently dispel the darkness of ignorance. This makes it necessary for a sixth example to show the endless work of Buddha activity. In the seventh example the wish-

fulfilling gem is solid, while the Buddha performs his activity while being completely non-existent creating a need for another example showing emptiness.

[375] The echo in the seventh example illustrates the non-existent quality but an echo must have a person and a rock to reflect the sound for an echo, while buddha activity is always present without any other conditions. So in the eighth example space is compared to buddha activity because it is always there and is naturally changeless, but one cannot say space is the source of all the good qualities that arise, while buddha activity is the ground from which all happiness and all good qualities of Buddhahood arise. So one needs the ninth example of the earth.

[376] The last example compares buddha activity with the earth showing that buddha activity is the ground from which all the qualities of enlightenment arise. Buddha activity is the ground from which the ultimate qualities of the Buddha, the levels of the bodhisattva, the qualities of meditation, and the immeasurable virtues of the Buddhas arise.

# CHAPTER 11

## *The Benefits of the Text*

[377] The *Uttara Tantra* shows that all beings possess buddha essence. How these qualities manifest, what qualities develop once enlightenment has been achieved, what qualities will develop from enlightenment, and how these qualities continue to help all sentient beings are the four points of the *Uttara Tantra*. These are called the four inconceivables because most beings, including bodhisattvas, cannot understand these points directly.

[378] These points are inconceivable but the wise, meaning those with intelligence, diligence, and faith, will become a vessel for the multitude of buddha qualities. To have great faith and sincere aspiration and an indirect idea of what these qualities are is a good condition because one becomes a vessel to achieve all the qualities of freedom and maturity of the Buddha. So the *Uttara Tantra* is like the first step towards realizing the qualities of a Buddha because it gives one the confidence that one can actually achieve enlightenment. Those who have interest in these qualities are planting the garden of delight in their minds and from these qualities all the virtues grow. It is the same as if one has planted a root which will give rise to a tree and grow. However, without planting a root, there is no hope of having a tree. Once one has planted a very strong root of virtue, it will grow until realization. Somebody with

this type of virtue surpasses the virtue of any other beings, because it's the virtue that will bring one to the qualities. Studying and meditating on the *Uttara Tantra* causes greater benefit than practicing generosity, skillful conduct, or patience.

The subject of this text is very precious because if someone studies this text, it will definitely help him or her reach Buddhahood. Although this text is inconceivable to ordinary beings, if one studies this teaching with faith and practices it accordingly, one will reach Buddhahood. In more detail:

[379] Suppose a bodhisattva practices great generosity to reach enlightenment. Every day he or she would make as many offerings of golden lands adorned with jewels as there are atoms in the buddha lands. If another bodhisattva just heard the words of this text and understood that this teaching is really a direct cause for reaching enlightenment and with faith and inspiration was moved to achieve enlightenment, this bodhisattva would have more virtue than the other bodhisattva who was making the offerings.

[380] A second example shows how even the virtue of keeping very pure moral conduct is eclipsed by the feeling of faith for this teaching. If a person aspires for enlightenment by keeping immaculate conduct of body, speech, and mind for eons and eons so that all bad actions are given up effortlessly were compared with a person inspired by this text, and had great enthusiasm, great joy, faith, and devotion, the virtue of the latter person would be much greater.

[381] Suppose someone had practiced meditative stability to extinguish the fire of defilements that leads to the existence in the three dimensions of saṃsāra and through

this meditation had extinguished the fire of these defilements. If this person were compared to someone studying and practicing this text, the benefits of studying and practicing the text would be greater than the practice of meditative stability.

[382] How is it possible that the virtue of simply hearing this teaching and feeling interest and faith in it would be greater than the virtue that comes from very great generosity, skillful conduct, or meditative stability? The answer is that generosity brings affluence, the practice of skillful conduct brings rebirth in higher realms, and the practice of meditation decreases defilements. The *Uttara Tantra*, however, teaches the inconceivable points which can lead to prajñā. The development of prajñā decreases one's obscurations and as a result one develops the understanding and the qualities of realization which are the first steps toward Buddhahood. Hearing this teaching and developing an interest in it will cause one to achieve Buddhahood so the development of prajñā is better than the development of other virtues.

There is a further benefit of this teaching. The *Uttara Tantra* teaches that there is buddha essence in all beings, but it is veiled by transitory obscurations. However, these can be removed so that enlightenment manifests. When this has happened there isn't a vacuum, but one develops full possession of the qualities of freedom and maturity. With the possession of these qualities, then spontaneously, effortlessly, and ceaselessly one will work for the benefit of all beings.

What is taught in the *Uttara Tantra* constitutes the exclusive domain of knowledge of all of the Buddhas. But if one hears this teaching and studies it, one will begin to understand that one already has the seed of Buddhahood in oneself and knowing this, one will be confident of becoming Buddha. So once one has heard this teaching and believed it, it would become the cause of becoming a Buddha. If one understands the four inconceivables, then this understanding will effortlessly give rise to the qualities of strong aspiration, diligence, mindfulness, meditative stability, prajñā, and so on. These qualities will arise spontaneously and the bodhicitta wish to achieve enlightenment to liberate all other beings will grow.

[388] Once we have understood these teachings, we won't fall back and the virtue we have accumulated will be brought to perfection by the practice of the other five pāramitās. This is because when we study this teaching with aspiration, we will develop a quality which is opposed to thinking in terms of "I" and "other." This teaching can then vanquish triplistic thought and by vanquishing these thoughts we will be made complete and pure.

[389] Through the five pāramitās of generosity, conduct, patience, meditation, and exertion virtue is gathered. The virtue that comes from generosity is gathered through giving; the virtue from skillful conduct is gathered by keeping very pure conduct; the virtue of meditative patience and meditative stability comes from practice; and the virtue that comes from exertion comes from diligence in practicing all other qualities.

[390] The next benefit of knowing this teaching and practicing it correctly is that it helps eliminate obscurations. The cognitive obscurations are those of triplistic thoughts, meaning that one divides all actions into a subject, object, and the action between them. For example, with generosity the outer object may be the poor

person, the subject may be a bodhisattva, and the action is what is given. Believing these links are real will make the generosity impure and create a cognitive obscuration. Emotional obscurations are negative thoughts such as those of greed which would prevent generosity. These obscurations keep us from enlightenment and with them, there is no way to achieve liberation. Even diligent practice of the pāramitās will not eliminate these obscurations. The only way to eliminate obscurations is through prajñā. This is why the practice of prajñā is so important. We can develop prajñā by studying sūtras or the śāstras on the profound teachings pertaining to absolute truth. This is why the cause for developing prajñā is the study of the profound topics and why studying the *Uttara Tantra* is so important.

### *How the Uttara Tantra was Composed*

[392] First, the *Uttara Tantra* was written by Asaṅga as a result of Buddha Maitreya's teachings. It was based on the words of the Buddha and written in accordance with the sūtras, particularly two sūtras about absolute truth.

Second, besides relying on the words of the Buddha, Asaṇga relied on logical reasoning to clarify doubts. He also used the direct cognition of the yogis. His purpose was to purify the buddha essence which is the very nature of the dharmakāya and help those who aspire to the mahāyāna path to achieve Buddhahood. One might think that if scriptural sources are used, one doesn't need to use logic. But a combination of both scriptures and logic is required. For example, if one looks at objects, one needs an external condition of a light of some sort such as the sun or a lamp and one needs an inner condition of good eyesight. It isn't enough to have just one condition. In the same way, a combination of the outer condition of knowledge of the meanings of the words and the inner condition of logical reasoning are needed to understand what the Buddha said.

Third, one needs to determine if one can trust these teachings of the Buddha. The teachings of the great sages remove all defilements connected with the three realms and show the benefit of peace. So, authentic teachings have to show the possibility of achieving nirvāṇa and be closely connected with the dharma. They should remove the defilements of all three dimensions of saṃsāra and should give peace of mind once liberation is achieved. A teaching without these characteristics wouldn't be the Buddha's teachings.

The śāstras, while not the Buddha's words, are worthy of respect and have the following characteristics. They should not be written out of a desire for fame, but written to help spread the teachings and help other beings on the path. Authors of the śāstras don't follow their fancy, but write with a completely unobstructed mind strictly in accordance with the Buddha's teachings. Their works also have the quality of being conducive to the path of liberation so it is possible through practicing the śāstras to achieve liberation because these teachings are in harmony with the conditions that lead to liberation. Because those who compose the śāstras have pure motivation and because the teachings are so close to what the Buddha said himself, they are worthy of being placed on one's head in the same way one would place the words of the Buddha himself.[9]

9 It is Tibetan custom that when one receives a religious object, one touches it to the top of one's head to receive a blessing from it.

[396] The Buddha has total knowledge of the nature of phenomena because of his complete purity. The bodhisattvas have many but not all of these characteristics. Whatever the Buddha taught in the sūtras shouldn't be adulterated, meaning one shouldn't say that this part of the teaching is correct, but that part is not. This would be mixing everything up and the true teaching would be destroyed.

[397] Since dharma is so valuable, it is very harmful to abandon it. One might give up the dharma by not understanding things the way they really are and therefore have contempt for the teachings. This happens because these persons are so attached to and involved their own ideas, that they can never change their minds. For example, one can dye a clean piece of cloth any color, but if it has grease stains on it, one can never dye it properly. In the same way, if the mind is clouded by fixed views even though it is exposed to the dharma, it just will not change its own ideas. This is an indirect cause for abandoning dharma.

[398] A more direct cause of not making spiritual progress is not having very good intelligence so that one does not understand the nature of phenomena. Another is the absence of an aspiration to goodness. Without this there's no wish to help other beings or to do anything good. When this aspiration is absent, everything becomes polluted and generates wrong views such as giving up the dharma. One may have great pride, boasting of qualities one doesn't possess. Or one may not have been exposed to dharma in a previous life and obviously not practiced much and as a result, one is quite heavily obscured by ignorance. The next cause is being so heavily obscured that one confuses the expedient meaning of the Buddha's teaching

with the absolute meaning or vice versa.

In addition, there are the six causes of wrong associations. If one associates closely with those who reject the dharma; if one avoids those who hold the teachings; if one has a low level of aspiration and enjoys things that are in contradiction with the dharma, then the teaching of the Buddha are likely to be abandoned. This is why one should know these causes and should try and eliminate them.

[399] Those who understand the dharma need not fear fire, venomous snakes, murderers, or lightning. One should instead fear losing the dharma because fire, snakes, murders, etc. can only make one lose one's life, but to lose the dharma causes the terrible sufferings of the lower realms and the suffering of saṃsāra. Therefore losing the teachings is more dangerous than anything else.

[400] If one associates very closely with friends who encourage one to do what is wrong, then very negative things will develop. Under this bad influence one may wish to kill the Buddha or kill one's own father, mother, or an arhat. One may also try to create a division among the saṅgha. These are the worst possible actions and are called the five actions of immediate result which means that when one dies, one falls immediately into the worst possible realm. There are even worse actions, but if one does these acts and then realizes the magnitude of these actions, one may use the four remedial powers to purify oneself and even reach liberation. So even these five very bad actions won't have such bad results if one is capable of purifying them. However, if one has wrong views of the dharma and dislikes it strongly in the short term, it doesn't seem so bad, but in the long-term it could be very dangerous because one will remain involved with outer things, not

seeing one's good qualities, and one may embark on the wrong path. Until one has given up the wrong attitude towards the dharma, one will never be able to reach liberation. If one never thinks in terms of reaching liberation, then one will never get there. This then is worse than committing the five actions of immediate results because with this attitude there is no prospect of ever obtaining liberation. This is why one must be careful of those who dislike of the dharma and those with wrong views.

***Dedication***

[401] The dedication is a wisdom prayer to Amitāyus and is also a summary of the whole text. It begins with the prayer that whatever virtue Maitreya has obtained through properly explaining these seven vajra points may all beings be able to meet Amitāyus who is the sage of boundless life and endowed with limitless life. To see him in his sambhogakāya form has a short-term benefit of having long life and a long-term benefit of being able to achieve perfect enlightenment once one's dharma eyes have been opened.

[402] Following is a recapitulation of this concluding chapter on the benefits of the text. The line "on what basis" refers to the first two lines of verse 392 stating the text was composed from the words of the Buddha and on the basis of logical reasoning. The two lines of this stanza answer the question "for which reasons" which is in order to purify oneself and to help other beings reach Buddhahood. The question "in which way" is answered in stanza 393 which states it was given by relying on the Buddha's teaching and

relying on Maitreya's understanding using the example of the necessity of light and eyes to see something properly. "That which has been explained" refers to stanza 394 on how to recognize a true Buddhist teaching and the śāstras which are defined in stanza 395.

[403] Next are the means for purifying oneself. One shouldn't change any of the Buddha's teachings and one should practice them as properly as possible (referring to stanzas 396 and 397). Then it refers to the causes for the loss of dharma (stanza 398) and what would be the results of this loss (stanzas 399 and 400). The immediate result is being reborn in a lower state, the ultimate result is being deprived of a choice for liberation for a long time.

[404] The last stanza of the text refers to the dedication (stanza 401) and shows the short-term and the long-term fruition. Through practice and dedication of virtue one can be born in the maṇḍala of the Buddha, see the sambhogakāya aspect of the Buddha, and therefore be able to see the true nature of everything and achieve supreme enlightenment. This shows that if one attains the relative level of enlightenment of a bodhisattva, one is in the company of the sambhogakāya Buddha and once the dharma eyes are opened, one achieves the ultimate level of enlightenment.

### *Summary*

We Buddhists have to follow the path outlined by the Buddha. We have to practice according to what the Buddha taught in the sūtras and the tantras and we should understand them just as they are. However, the sūtras sometimes were answers to a given situation or a disciple's particular question and sometimes the Buddha would answer questions based on the understanding suitable to his audience at the time. So sometimes the sūtras were quite difficult to understand because some passages are extremely clear and others less clear. Also a sūtra would specialize in a particular topic so if one wanted to know the general concepts of Buddhism, one had to read sūtras scattered throughout various books. This is why most Buddhists in Tibet resorted to studying the śāstras. These made the deeper meaning of Buddha's words more accessible and they didn't change the meaning of the dharma. This is why the śāstras were so extremely important.

The *Uttara Tantra* was composed by Maitreya who was no ordinary being because he is a representative of the Buddhas and will be the next Buddha in our world. So he is the most superior author of the śāstra that one could find. The *Uttara Tantra* was translated from Sanskrit to Tibetan by the great scholar Sadzana who was the nephew of Brahmin Ratnavajra, he who was from the "City of Glory" which we believe is the city of Śrīnagarī, but we are not completely sure. It was also translated in that same City of Glory by the Tibetan monk Loden Sherab.

# Glossary

## *Technical Terms used in this Text*

**abhidharma** (Tib. *chö ngön pa*) The Buddhist teachings are often divided into the sūtras (the teachings of the Buddha), the vinaya (teachings on conduct) and the abhidharma (the analysis of phenomena).

**absolute truth** (Skt. paramārtha satya Tib. *dondam*) There are two truths or views of reality—relative truth which is seeing things as ordinary beings do with the dualism of "I" and "other" and absolute truth, also called ultimate truth, which is transcending duality and seeing things as they are.

**arhats** (Tib. *dra chom pa*) Accomplished hinayāna practioners who have eliminated the kleśa obscurations. They are fully realized śrāvakas and pratyekabuddha.

**bhūmi** (Tib. *sa*) The levels or stages a bodhisattva goes through to reach enlightenment. Also called the bodhisattva levels and usually described as consisting of ten levels in the sūtra tradition and 13 in the tantra tradition.

**bodhicitta** (Tib. *chang chup chi sem*) Literally, the mind of enlightenment. There are two kinds of bodhicitta—absolute or completely awakened mind that sees the emptiness of phenomena and relative bodhicitta which is the aspiration to practice the six pāramitās and free all beings from the sufferings of saṃsāra.

**bodhisattva** (Tib. *chang chup sem pa*) An person who has committed him or herself to the mahāyāna path of compassion and the practice of the six pāramitās to free beings from saṃsāra.

**buddha nature** (Sk. tathāgatagarbha, Tib. *deshin shekpai nying po*) The original nature present in all beings which when realized leads to enlightenment. It is often called the essence of Buddhahood or enlightened essence and is the topic of the *Uttara Tantra*.

**Buddha Śākyamuni** The Buddha, often called the Gautama Buddha, who is the latest Buddha and lived between 563 and 483 B. C.

**buddhakāyas** See kāyas.

**cakravartin** (Tib. *khor lo gur pa*) A cakravartin, also called a universal monarch, is a king who propagates the dharma and starts a new era.

**Cittamātra school** (Tib. *sem tsampa*) A school founded by Asaṅga in the fourth century and is usually translated as the Mind Only School. It is one of the four major schools in the mahāyāna tradition and its main tenet (to greatly simplify) is that all phenomena are mental events.
**clear light** (Skt. *prabhāsvara*, Tib. *ösel*) A subtle state of mind and according to tantric teachings is the state of mind that highest realization is attained.
**dharma** (Tib. *chō*) Dharma has two main meanings: Any truth such as the sky is blue; second, as it is used in this text, the teachings of the Buddha (also called buddhadharma).
**dharma of realization** (Tib. *tog pa chō*) The dharma teachings which have been derived from direct realization. These contrast with dharma of statements.
**dharma of statements** (Tib. *lung gi-chō*) Teachings based on the Buddhist scriptures. Also called scriptural dharma or the teachings of the Tripiṭaka.
**dharmacakra** (Skt. for "wheel of dharma," Tib. *chō chi khor lo* ) The Buddha's teachings correspond to three levels: the hīnayāna, the mahāyāna and the vajrayāna with each set being one turning of the wheel of dharma.
**dharmadhātu** (Tib. *chō ying*) The all-encompassing space which is unoriginated and without beginning out of which all phenomena arise. The Sanskrit means "the essence of phenomena" and the Tibetan means "the expanse of phenomena" but usually it refers to the emptiness which is the essence of phenomena.
**dharmakāya** (Tib. *chō ku*) One of the three bodies of buddhahood. It is enlightenment itself, that is wisdom beyond reference point. See kāyas, three.
**dharmatā** (Tib. *chō nyi*) Dharmatā is often translated as "suchness" or "the true nature of things" or "things as they are." It is phenomena as it really is or as seen by a completely enlightened being without any distortion or obscuration so one can say it is "reality."
**eight mental fabrications** Not having the eight mental fabrications is to be without a beginning, without a cessation, without nihilism, without eternalism, without going, without coming, not being separate, and not being non-separate.
**five actions of immediate result** These actions such as killing one's guru which cause one to be reborn immediately in the hell realm upon death.

**five aggregrates** (Skt. skandha, Tib. *pung po nga*) Literally "heaps" are the five basic transformations that perceptions undergo when an object is perceived. These are form, feeling, perception, formation, and consciousness.

**five levels of practice** See paths, five.

**form kāyas** (Sk. rūpakāya) The sambhogakāya and the nirmāṇakāya.

**four extremes** These are a belief in the existence of everything ("eternalism"), a belief that nothing exists ("nihilism"), a belief that things exist and don't exist, and a belie. that reality is something other than existence and non-existence.

**four fearlessnesses** (Skt. *catvāravāiśāradya*, Tib. *mi jig pa*) The four stages to be attained by bodhisattvas. They are being fearless in abandoning all faults, fearless of complete realization, fearless in showing the path to others, and fearless in pointing out obscurations on the path.

**four inconceivables or immeasurables** (Skt. *catvāry apramāṇāni*, Tib. *tsad med pa*) The four qualities that one achieves with complete enlightenment. Being inconceivable to ordinary persons they are loving kindness, compassion, joy, and equanimity.

**four noble truths** (Tib. *pak pay den pa shi*) The first teaching of the Buddha and the foundation of Buddhism. These are the truth of suffering, the truth of the cause of suffering, the truth of the cessation of suffering, and the eightfold path to enlightenment.

**four particularities** These are the characteristics of buddha nature when it manifests as complete enlightenment. They are lucid clarity, purity, possessing characteristics of enlightenment, and the presence of nonconceptual and analytical judgement.

**four unfavorable obstacles** The four obstacles in reaching complete enlightenment are a dislike of the dharma, a strong belief in self, fear of suffering on the path, and lack of motivation to help others.

**ground, path, and fruition** A logical method for describing something used in many Buddhist works. First one describes the causal conditions (ground), then the coming together of these causes towards some goal (path), and finally the result (fruition).

**hīnayāna** (Tib. *tek pa chung wa*) Literally means "the lesser vehicle" which refers to the first teachings of the Buddha such as the four noble truths that developed into the 18 early schools of Buddhism. Also called the Theravādin path.

**how-it-is** see knowledge of how-it-is.

**hungry ghosts** (Skt. preta, Tib. *yidak* ) A type of being who is always starved for food and water. See the six realms of saṃsāra.

**jñāna** (Tib. *yeshe*) Enlightened wisdom which is beyond dualistic thought.

**Kagyu** (Tib.) One of the four major schools of Buddhism in Tibet headed by His Holiness Karmapa. The other three schools are the Nyingmapas, the Sākyas, and the Gelupas.

**kalpa** (Tib. *kal pa*) An eon which lasts in the order of millions of years.

**karma** (Tib. *lay*) Literally means "action" and karma is a natural law stating that when one does a wholesome action, one's circumstances will improve; when one does an un-wholesome action negative results will eventually occur from the act.

**kāyas, three** (Tib. *ku*) The three bodies of the Buddha: the nirmāṇakāya, sambhogakāya and dharmakāya. The dharmakāya (the "truth body"), is the complete enlightenment of the Buddha which is unoriginated wisdom beyond form and manifests in the sambhogakāya and the nirmāṇakāya. The sambhogakāya (the "enjoyment body"), manifests only to bodhisattvas. The nirmāṇakāya (the "emanation body") manifests in the ordinary world and in the context of the *Uttara Tantra* manifests as the Śākyamuni Buddha.

**kleśa** (Tib. *nyōn mong*) These are the emotional (in contrast to intellectual) obscurations and are often called "mind poison" and translated as "defilements" in this text. The three main poisons are ataachment (also translated as desire), aggression (anger or adversion) and ignorance (or delusion). The five poisons are these three plus pride and jealousy.

**knowledge of how-it-is** (Tib. *ji ta ba*) This is transcendent knowledge of the true nature of reality, not as it appears to individuals in saṃsāra.

**knowledge of variety** (Tib. *ji nye pa*) This is the transcendent knowledge of the variety of reality.

**luminosity** (Tib. *sal wa*) In the vajrayāna everything is void, but this voidness is not completely empty because it has luminosity. Luminosity or luminous clarity allows all phenomena to appear and is a characteristic of emptiness (Skt. śūnyatā).

**lung** A Tibetan word for ritual reading. To perform a vajrayāna practice, one must have a holder of the lineage read the text through (Tib. *lung*), give an explanation of the practice (Tib. *tri*) and give the empowerment for the practice (Tib. *wang*).

**madhyamaka** (Tib. *u ma*) A philosophical school often called the Middle Way school founded by Nāgārjuna in the 2nd century. The main principle of this school is proving that everything is devoid of any inherent independent reality, that is, the teachings of emptiness.
**mahāmudrā** (Tib. *cha ja chen po*) Literally means "great seal" and is the meditative transmission handed down especially by the Kagyu school.
**mahāpaṇḍita** A great Buddhist scholar (paṇḍita).
**mahāyāna** (Tib. *tek pa chen po*) Literally means "great vehicle" and are the teachings of the second and third turning of the wheel of dharma that teach the path of a bodhisattva, compassion for all beings, and realization of emptiness.
**Maitreya** In this work this refers to the Bodhisattva Maitreya who lived at the time of the Buddha.
**māra** (Tib. *dud*) Difficulties encountered by the practitioner. There are four kinds—skandhamāra which is incorrect view of self, kleśamāra which is being overpowered by negative emotions, mṛtyumāra which is death and interrupts spiritual practice, and devaputramāra which is becoming stuck in the bliss that comes out of meditation.
**mind only** school. See Cittamātra.
**nirmāṇakāya**. See kāyas.
**nirvāṇa** (Tib. *nya ngen lay day pa*) Literally, "extinction" (of ignorance) and means liberation from saṃsāra and suffering.
**paṇḍita** A great scholar.
**pāramitās** In Sanskrit it means "perfections." These are the six practices of the mahāyāna path: Perfection of generosity (dāna), of discipline (śīla), of patience (kṣānti), of exertion (vīrya), of meditation (dhyāna), and of knowledge (prajñā)
attachment, aggression and ignorance.
**paths, five** Traditionally, a practitioner goes through five stages or paths to enlightenment. These are The Path of Accumulation (Skt. sambhāramārga) which emphasizes purifying one's obscurations and accumulating merit. The Path of Junction or Application (Skt. prayogamārga) in which the meditator develops profound understanding of the four noble truths and cuts the root to the desire realm. The Path of Insight or Seeing (Sk. darśanamārga) in which the meditator develops greater insight and enters the first bodhisattva level. The Path of Meditation (Skt. bhāvanamārga) in which the meditator cultivates insight in the 2nd through 10th bodhisattva levels. And the

Path of Fulfillment (Skt. aśaiksammārga) which is the complete attainment of buddhahood.

**poisons, three** The three poisons or major defilements also called desire or attachment, anger or aggression, and ignorance or bewilderment.

**prajñā** (Tib. *she rab*) In Sanskrit it means "perfect know-ledge" and can mean wisdom, understanding, intelligence, discrimination, or judgement according to context.

**pratyekabuddha** (Tib. *rang sang gay*) Literally means "solitary realizer" and in this text it is a realized hīnayāna practitioner who has achieved the jñāna of how-it-is and variety, but who has not committed him or herself to the bodhisattva path of helping others.

**ratna** (Tib. *rin po che*) Literally, a jewel but in this context refers to the three jewels which are the Buddha, the dharma, and the saṅgha.

**relative truth** (Tib. *kunsop*) There are two truths: relative and absolute. Relative truth is the perception of an ordinary (unenlightened) person who sees the world with all his or her projections based on a false belief in ego.

**rinpoche** Literally, "very precious" and is used as a term of respect for a Tibetan guru.

**salwa** Tibetan for luminosity. In the vajrayāna everything is void, but this voidness is not completely empty because it has luminosity. Luminosity or clarity allows all phenomena to appear and is a characteristic of emptiness (śūnyatā).

**samādhi** (Tib. *ting nge dzin*) An advanced state in which the mind is in one-pointed meditation. It is also called "meditative absorpiton.

**śamatha** (Tib. *shi nay*) See tranquility meditation.

**saṅgha** (Tib. *gen dun*) These are the companions on the path. They may be all the persons on the path or the noble saṅgha which are the realized ones.

**sambhogakāya** See the three kāyas.

**saṃsāra** (Tib. *kor wa*) Conditioned existence which is characterized by suffering in ordinary life because one is still afflicted by attachment, aggression, and ignorance.

**samvrtikāya** There is the body of ultimate truth (Skt. paramārthakāya) and the body of relative truth (Skt. samvrtikāya). This is the embodiment in relative truth.

**śāstra** (Tib. *ten chö*) The Buddhist teachings are divided into words of the Buddha (the sūtras) and the commentaries by others on the

Buddha's works (śāstras).

**six realms of saṃsāra** The possible types of rebirths for beings in saṃsāra: the god realm in which gods have great pride, the asura realm in which the jealous gods try to maintain what they have, the human realm which is the best realm because one has the possiblity of achieving enlightenment, the animal realm characterized by stupidity, the hungry ghost realm characterized by great craving, and the hell realms characterized by aggression.

**śrāvakas** (Tib. *nyon thos*) Literally "those who hear" meaning disciples. A type of realized hīnayāna practioner (arhat) who has achieved the realization of the nonexistence of personal self.

**stūpa** (Tib. *chō ten*) A dome shaped monument to the Buddha which often contains relics and remains of the Buddha or great bodhisattvas.

**sugatagarbha** (Tib. *der sheg nying po*) Buddha nature or that enlightened essence present in all beings that allows them to have the capacity to achieve enlightenment. It is closely related to tathagātagarbha.

**śūnyatā** (Tib. *tong pa nyi*) Usually translated as "voidness" or "emptiness." In the second turning of the wheel of dharma the Buddha taught that external phenomena and internal phenomena are devoid of any real inherent existence.

**sūtra** (Tib. *do*) These are the hinayanā and mabayanā teachings which are the words of the Śākyamuni Buddha. They are often contrasted with the śāstras.

**supreme yogi** An epithet for the Buddha.

**svābhāvikakāya** Refers to the dharmakāya of the Buddha.

**tathāgatas** Literally, those who have gone to "thatness." A title of the Buddhas.

**tathātagatagarbha** (Tib. *de shin shek pay nying po*) This is the seed or essence of tathata (suchness) and is also called buddha essence or enlightened essence.

**ten powers of the Buddha** These are special "miraculous" powers of the Buddha.

**terma** Literally means "hidden treasure" and are works hidden by great bodhisattvas and later rediscovered. They might be actual physical texts or they may come from "the sky" as transmissions from the sambhogakāya.

**three jewels** (Tib. *kön chok sum*) These are the Buddha, the dharma, and the saṅgha.

**three marks of existence** These are the characteristics of impermanent objects and mean an object has a beginning, it has a solid existence in the present, and it decays or disintegrates into smaller constituents in the future.

**tīrthikas** Religious people who believe in a personal self. Also referred to as icchantikas.

**tranquility meditation** (Sk. śamatha, Tib. *shi nay*) A basic meditation practice aimed at taming and sharpening the mind. It is also called basic sitting meditation.

**Tripitaka** Literally, the "three baskets." These are the sūtras (the narrative teachings of the Buddha), the vinaya (a code for monks and nuns) and the abhidharma (philosophical background of the dharma).

**triplistic thought** Is believing in the solidity of relative reality by dividing all actions into subject and object and the exchange between the two. For example, on the relative level, one (subject) does a prostration (the action between) to a buddha statue (object).

**Tuṣita heaven** This is one of the heaven fields of the Buddha. Tuṣita is in the sambhogakāya and therefore is not located in any place or time.

**twelve deeds of the Buddha** Traditionally the Buddha per-formed 12 major deeds in his life.

**upāya** (Tib. *tab)* The skillful means used by enlightened beings to present the dharma taking the person's capabilities and propensities into account.

**vajra** (Tib. *dorje*) In Sanskrit a "thunderbolt" which was a weapon of Indra. In Tibet it generally means anything invincible or indestructible or "diamond-like."

**vajrayāna** (Tib. *dorje tek pa*) One of the three major traditions of Buddhism (the hīnayāna, the mahāyāna and the vajrayāna). The vajrayāna was based on the tantras and became the major tradition of Tibet.

**victorious one** One of the epitaths given to the Buddha.

**vinaya** (Tib. *dul wa*) The teachings of the Buddha concerning proper conduct. There are seven main precepts that may be observed by lay persons or various levels of monks and nuns.

**wheel of dharma** (Skt. *dharmacarka*) The Buddha's teachings correspond to three levels: the hīnayāna, the mahāyāna, and the vajrayāna with each set being one turning.

**yāna** (Tib. *tek pa* ) Literally, a "vehicle" but in this text refers to a level of teaching. There are three main yānas (see hīnayāna, mahāyāna, and vajrayāna).

## *Appendix A*

| Pronounced | Transliteration | English |
|---|---|---|
| chang chub | byang chub | enlightenment |
| chang chub sem pa | byang chub sems dpa' | bodhisattva |
| chang chub sem | byang chub sems | bodhicitta |
| ching wa | bying ba | bondage |
| chö | chos | dharma |
| chö kyi yang | chos kyi dbyings | dharmadhātu |
| chöten | mchod rten | stūpa |
| der sheg nying po | bde gshegs snying po | buddha nature |
| de shin shek pe nying po | de bzhin gsheg pai'nyingpo | tathātagharba |
| dondam | don dam bden pa | absolute truth |
| dorje | rdo rje | vajra |
| dri | khrid | explanation |
| duma che | 'dusma byas | uncreated |
| gendun | dge 'dun | saṅgha |
| gyü lama | rgyud bla ma | *Uttara Tantra* |
| ji nye pa | ji snyed pa | kn. of variety |
| ji ta ba | ji lta ba | kn. how-it-is |
| kern cho | dkon mchog | three jewels |
| ku | sku | kāya (body) |
| kun zop | kun rdzob | relative truth |
| lung | lung | ritual reading |
| lung gi chö | lung gi chos | dhar statements |
| mi ji pa | mi' jigs pa | 4 fearlessnesses |
| mu tek pa | mu stegs pa | tīrthikas |

| Pronounced | Transliteration | English |
|---|---|---|
| nang gi yeshe | nang gi ye shes | inner jnana |
| ngon she | mngon shes | clear cognition |
| non mong | nyon mongs | kleśa |
| ösel | 'od gsal | clear light |
| pag pa | 'phags pa | realized |
| rinpoche | rin po che | precious jewel |
| salwa | gsal ba | luminosity |
| sang gye | sangs rgyas | Buddha |
| sherab | shes rab | prajñā |
| shi nay | zhi gnas | śamatha |
| tan cho | bstan bcos | śāstra |
| teg pa | theg pa | yāna |
| teg pa chen po | theg pa chen po | mahāyāna |
| terma | gterma | treasure |
| tog pa chö | rtogs pa'i chos | dh. realization |
| tong pa nyi | stong pa nyid | dh. statements |
| wang | dbang | empowerment |
| yeshe | ye shes | jñāna |